# OUTRAGE

## An Anarchist Memoir of the Penal Colony

# OUTRAGE

## An Anarchist Memoir of the Penal Colony

Clément Duval

Translated by Michael Shreve

Introduction by Marianne Enckell

*Outrage: An Anarchist Memoir of the Penal Colony*
Michael Shreve © 2012
This edition © 2012 PM Press

ISBN: 978-1-60486-500-4
LCCN: 2011939693

PM Press
P.O. Box 23912
Oakland, CA 94623
pmpress.org

10 9 8 7 6 5 4 3 2 1

Cover by John Yates
Layout by Jonathan Rowland

This book has been made possible in part by a generous donation from the Anarchist Archives Project.

Printed on recycled paper by the Employee Owners of Thomson-Shore in Dexter, Michigan.
www.thomsonshore.com

# Contents

# Introduction to the English Edition

The last Frenchmen who had been sentenced to the penal colony in Guiana were not repatriated until 1954, a century after the Second Empire had adopted the "Loi sur l'exécution de la peine des travaux forcés" (Law on the execution of the sentence of hard labor). Starting in 1852 more than seventy thousand men were sent to Guiana: at least three fourths died there; barely five thousand made it back to France freed; nine thousand escaped—there were very few survivors.

Clément Duval was one of them. Condemned in 1887 to hard labor for life, he managed to leave "l'enfer vert" (the green hell) after fourteen years and eighteen escape attempts. In his *Memoir* he tells about this hope that was stronger than everything he had to put up with: hunger, sickness, the constant humiliations inflicted on the convicts.

Duval was not a hero, nor was he a victim of a miscarriage of justice: he was an anarchist who admitted his crimes—breaking and entering, burglary, wounding a police officer—and bore his sentence. But he continuously protested against the abuses, arbitrary punishments, guards' contempt, snitching, cheating, and blatant injustices against the weakest or most rebellious.

Many anarchists ended up in the penal colonies after the "lois scélérates " (villainous laws) of 1892 allowed convictions for crimes of opinion or inciting violence. In France, from 1892 to 1894, Ravachol, Vaillant, Émile Henry, and Caserio paid for their crimes with their heads. Accomplices, a few imitators, and comrades with ideas judged to be "particularly dangerous" were sent to Guiana. They had put up posters or insulted a police officer, they sang subversive songs or bragged about living without working … The English sent boys suspected of stealing a handkerchief to mysterious Australia.

Off the shores of Cayenne, the administrative center of Guiana and a name emblematic of the penal colony, were the Salvation Islands: Devil's Island, reserved for those convicted of high treason like Captain Dreyfus, Saint Joseph Island and Royal Island for the "troublemakers"—the recidivists, repeat offenders. The penal colony was not a mere matter of breaking rocks in a faraway land. It was a system that was highly refined in brutality, in wasting lives and money, in the maniacal control over the lives of convicts so that every minute was a punishment. They called it "the dry guillotine."

The system quickly destroyed whoever was caught up in its gears, whether they were convicts or bureaucrats. Betrayal and shady deals dominated both sides. The hierarchical chain held the men as tightly as the shackles—it rotted their flesh and spirit. The promotion of convicts to the rank of foreman (contremaître) reinforced it: the foremen had to be the biggest toughs, the biggest snitches, and the biggest bootlickers because at the least offense they would be sent back among the crowd of convicts where their hopes of survival were slim.

See, when you're caught, it's forever. Someone sentenced to eight years or more of hard labor had to "double" it, that is, stay in the colony for the same amount of time. He rarely survived, let alone earned enough money to finance a trip back to France. Most of the convicts (just like today) were young men. Some would live twenty, thirty, even fifty years dressed in shabby clothes, eating rancid bacon and rotten vegetables—crippled, sick, and powerless. A life of answering "present" twice a day at roll call, screaming your name and number at every passing of the guard, suffering the insults and humiliations in silence, stashing away whatever might bear witness to another life: a photograph, a letter ... with time in the hole for a trifle or a murder, for a bag of tobacco or a failed escape.

Clément Duval resisted. Born in 1850, he was older than most of his comrades. He was in the war of 1870 and had already known a hard life. But above all he was an anarchist and proud of it. A locksmith by trade, he refused to make handcuffs or sharpen the guillotine. When the director threatened to make him bend to his will, he answered "that mindful men, such as I considered myself, were like glass—they might break, but they never bend."

When the big convoys of anarchists started arriving in Cayenne in 1892, Duval had already been there for five years. He had earned the respect of a few guards and the express animosity of others. He knew the possibilities of "making stuff" to earn a few extra sous or a little trust. He was aware of the risks of ill-prepared escape attempts. He knew who were the "stubborn mules" to watch out for. A dozen anarchists sentenced between 1892 and 1894 died from sickness or in revolt the same year they got there; a dozen died while trying to escape, or when too old to escape; four went back to France. Only two bore witness, Clément Duval and Auguste Liard-Courtois. If it weren't for the publication of their memoirs, most of the others would have remained anonymous. (Short biographies are included in this book.)

❊   ❊   ❊

Duval's *Memoir* began appearing in 1907 in the Italian anarchist weekly *Cronaca Sovversiva* in New York. Duval arrived in New York in 1903 and was taken care of by the Italian anarchist comrades, a large, united colony. Luigi Galleani, who had personally known the penal colony in the Italian islands, welcomed him in his home and started working on a translation of his manuscript—really, an interpretation: he did not hesitate to rewrite entire dialogues and descriptions in order to enhance the text and create a thousand-page tome that was published in 1929 by the Biblioteca dell'Adunata dei Refrattari.

Luigi Galleani died in 1931 in Italy, Clément Duval in 1935 in Brooklyn at the age of eighty-five. The children of the Italian anarchists gradually integrated into American society and *L'Adunata dei refrattari*, one of their principal newspapers, shut down in 1971. The last editor, Max Sartin, was the one who left me Clément Duval's manuscript in 1980.

Max was a worthy heir of the illegalists. He lived under a false name, had his mail sent to neighbors (who offered me a plate of homemade tortellini and California wine as good as any Italian wine) and it was not until our second meeting that he let me in his house in Brooklyn to give me a glimpse of his archives. And, in the end, to give me a thick envelope marked "CD."

His companion Fiorina and he led me to the subway with strong advice, and I did not dare open the envelope before being in a safe place. There were more than four hundred pages of manuscript there and a large photo of Duval. I did not know at the time that he had spent his final years with them. But I did know that since Galleani, no one had looked at those pages and no extract had been published in French.

In the following years I transcribed the manuscript and verified (unfortunately) that the missing pages were definitely lost. I spent time in the archives of the penal colony in Aix-en-Provence, in a dusty attic where huge registers contained what remains of prisoners' lives: administrative reports, lists of sentences and escape attempts, seized letters … I was able to fish out a few names that Duval only knew by ear (he wrote Kervaux for Thiervoz, Paridaine for Paridaën), tie in a few facts, and dig up a little supplementary information. Then I read everything published about the penal colony (the books have multiplied since then), even the so-called *Memoirs* of Papillon, the anti-Duval par excellence: not only was most of his book made up, but he constantly bragged about being friendly with the prison administration, he denounced his comrades, he saved a guard's little girl, he complacently surrendered to the most humiliating and degrading jobs … His fantastic escape attempts were often borrowed from legend; he showed no solidarity with the other prisoners and no political conscience, the exact opposite of Duval, or Alexandre Jacob, or Jacob Law.

❊   ❊   ❊

The text published here represents the bulk of the manuscript. The punctuation has been standardized, the spelling regularized, and the chapters organized, but otherwise it is unchanged (translator's notes are enclosed in brackets). The French publisher found the original too long and it was necessary to sacrifice several of the repetitive passages. It is not essential in reading to feel the same pestering boredom, day after day, year after year, and the failures that happen over and over again. We are not talking about a literary work here, even if Duval did his best to shape it up. What we have here is an eyewitness account of the absurdity of the repressive system and ways to resist it, and the persistence of anarchist values in one of the most hostile environments that ever existed.

—Marianne Enckell
(translated by Michael Shreve)

# Chapter 1
# I Rebelled Because It Was My Right

January 1887. Brief summary of the examination:

After the usual formalities—the comedy—first and last names, occupation, etc. I was accused of robbery, arson, and attempted murder.

"In 1878 you were sentenced to one year in prison."

"Yes, and I take full responsibility for this conviction."

"In 1883 you were sentenced to forty-eight hours in jail for rebellion against police officers."

"Yes, I rebelled against your police because it was my right."

"You stand accused of illegal entry, of breaking and entering into the residence of Madame Lemaire, a person of private means, and taking from her fifteen thousand francs' worth of jewelry on the night of October 4, 1886."

"Yes, parasites should not have jewelry when the workers, the producers do not have bread. I have only one regret: that I did not find the money that I was intending to use for revolutionary propaganda, otherwise I would not be here in the hot seat, but busy making devices to blow you all up."

"The prosecution has shown that you had an accomplice and you said that his name was Turquais and that he was in England to sell the jewelry. This Turquais is a figment of your imagination or else tell us where he is."

"Let your snitches go look for him!"

"Didier and Houchard are your accomplices."

"No. Both are completely unaware of the provenance of the brooch I gave Houchard to sell as a jeweler since I needed money right away for … He's an idiot, he used go-betweens and he's the reason I'm here."

"The pliers they found were rather extraordinary. You said to the examining judge that you made them yourself."

"Yes, I also said that I had made them a long time ago, I was just waiting for the right time to use them because I had been convinced for a long time that the workers were powerless to fight with their own resources and that only on the day when they would have the courage to smash the safes of their masters and exploiters would they come out of the struggle victorious …"

Bérard des Glajeux, the presiding judge, rattled his bell because he did not want to listen to such truths anymore and he threatened to throw me out for proudly proclaiming in open court the right to steal. The rat, he knew better than anyone that I was invoking the right to insurrection. Yes! In this century of the worship of the Golden Calf all means are good for anarchists to bring about the triumph of the grand ideal of social renovation and regeneration based on liberty, equality, morality, and justice. Yes, rotten and corrupted bourgeoisie, your gold is needed to wage war against you, to annihilate forever the class struggle of which it is the main cause, and not to enjoy it. Vile metal that we despise and will destroy after the struggle, just like the qualifications of private income and property, in order to share between everyone. That is what I had to say, which Bérard did not want to hear.

"So, for you it wasn't robbery?"

"No, it was a just restitution. This money, I repeat, was bound to be used for revolutionary propaganda. I know only two kinds of theft: theft through the exploitation of man by man in business—legal theft; and that which strips the bourgeoisie, the thieves, in order to enjoy it instead of them. But then that thief in turn becomes a parasite and consequently an enemy. That's who the thieves are. As for me, no one who has known me closely since my youth will criticize me for any dishonest act. But to serve the revolution—I got over all kinds of prejudices a long time ago.

"You were demoted from the rank of corporal for insubordination."

"I was named corporal in spite of myself and a bunch of times I wanted to turn in my stripes, but they wouldn't let me. See, at the time I was an anarchist without knowing the theories, only through natural common sense—I hated authority. You criticize me for having been demoted from the rank of corporal, but you don't talk about the two wounds I got during the war, idiot that I was! Just like the rheumatism, an awful sickness, that I got in that murderous comedy of 1870 [against the Prussians]."

"You are accused of having set fire, in two different places, to the residence of Madame Lemaire on the night of October 4. You told the investigating judge that it was Turquais who lit the two fires and that you had done everything possible to prevent him from doing this, your reason being that it was a nice, very comfortable house and that you should keep it safe for the day of the Revolution when the workers would leave their slums, and that in this house there was room for eight or ten families to live there comfortably. But being angry that he did not find what he was looking for he didn't want to listen to you and avenged himself by trying to harm the parasites who lived in the house."

The Presiding Judge: "It is an act of horrendous vandalism."

"Yes, those are the reasons I gave to Turquais before he lit the fire because the parasites weren't in the house to be grilled. But don't think because of this that I renounce arsonists. On the contrary, I approve of the labor slave who burns the prison where they exploit him; by this he destroys the symbol of servitude and slavery ..."

My last words were not heard by the public. Glajeux rattled his bell and spoke so loudly to shut me up that he drowned out my voice.

"You are accused of the attempted murder of Sergeant Rossignol. When this officer was investigating Didier with the chief of detectives, Didier's wife pointed you out as Duval to the officer. He asked you to follow him to talk to the chief of detectives. You answered that you had no business with him and he wasn't one of your friends. Seeing this, the officer identified himself as a sergeant of the police and arrested you in the name of the law. You answered him: 'Ah! Scum, in the name of freedom I'll strike you down!' And you stabbed him eight times with a handmade dagger, intending to kill him."

"I only struck Sergeant Rossignol twice and not eight times. If I'd stabbed him eight times, being all worked up by the surprise at being arrested as I was, he would probably not be here to testify. It was a scratch, a scrape that he got when we fell off the sidewalk. Unfortunately, he dragged me down with him in his fall, otherwise neither he nor Officer Pelletier, who was with him, would have arrested me."

"So, you would have killed them both?"

"No, I would have defended my freedom. But I couldn't. Officer Pelletier right away took advantage of my fall by grabbing me by my throat and my private parts; and Rossignol was able too get hold of my right thumb and bite it."

❖ ❖ ❖

Mr. [Fernand] Labori summoned two comrades who knew me closely, Ricois and Bronsin, but both refused to take the oath and raise their hand before the image of Rufano [it most probably means Christ, but the signification has not been found]. At Labori's request Bérard postponed the hearing for ten minutes. Labori went to talk with my two friends, but they remained firm in their convictions.

When the hearing resumed, my comrade Ricois was called first. Des Glajeux then read in a fat tome that in accordance with such and such article of the law, for refusing the oath, the court fined him one hundred francs.

Then I yelled to him, "Hey, Ricois, aren't you going to say thank you? You see these people here, they don't need to break down doors to get money. In accordance with such and such article of the law and there you go, one hundred francs!"

He answered, "What do you expect? The government of the bourgeois Republic needs money."

Then it was the turn of my comrade Bronsin, who is very deaf and made Glajeux repeat his request two or three times. Then you should have seen all those slimy individuals, all those hacks of the bourgeois and re-actionary press make fun of the old man's, the old worker's disability. You have no idea how painful it was for me not to be able to avenge the insult given to this worthy and loyal friend. Ah! If those four henchmen weren't next to me …

"So, do you want to raise your hand and take the oath?"

"No, I formally refuse. Ask me whatever you want about Duval, his public or private life, I'll answer you. But to raise my hand before this image? Never!"

Like Ricois, he was fined one hundred francs. Bronsin is a sixty-nine-year-old man with a white beard and white hair, a very good gunsmith, sought out even by the exploiters when he was young. But when your beard and hair turn white, you are no longer respected by the moneyed people with whom you collaborated. "I don't need you anymore, lowlife worker, despicable mob, go, go now and die like a dog in a hole somewhere." That is what happened to Bronsin after a dozen years working for the same ex-ploiter—after he had made its fortune. The son took over the shop and soon afterward informed our friend that he had to find another job, not that he had complaints about his work, but because he was too impassioned; and then he started insulting the socialists and revolutionaries. Bronsin is an extremely loyal man, the most honest I know. He told me sometimes, "I would like to live in a glass house so that the actions of my life could be checked." I want to show our friend's character because I think that the police will have a sorry welcome when they show up to collect the 100 franc fine. Moreover, I love to talk about him; I love him like a father.

※   ※   ※

[The next day] Mr. Renaud, the prosecutor, took the floor. I cannot complain about him much. He played his role pretty well. He said that it was very lucky that I fell into the hands of justice since I was, as I had said the day before, a man of action, capable of using dynamite and the most lethal devices to serve the anarchist ideal; that he was dealing with utopia because he saw the progress that this noble ideal was making, so goodbye to all kinds of privileges. Like his fellow bourgeoisie he was scared. Not being able to smear me in my public or private life, he treated me as an enemy of society (of the current society, he was right). He concluded by asking for my head and almost for the acquittal of Houchard and Didier, my two codefendants.

I asked to speak in response—formal refusal by Bérard.

The floor was given to Mr. Labori and he made a great speech for the defense. From the newspaper *Le Révolté* he read several letters of comrades expressing their solidarity with the act that had put me in the hot seat, since they knew my motive and goal. He dealt with the anarchist theories pretty well. Even though he did not share our ideal, he found it noble and grand, but he was bourgeois—there was a conflict of interests: he owned things and did not want to lose them.

I made his job easy because I had given him my whole life story.

Bérard des Glajeux asked me if I had something to say after my defense attorney's plea and before the Court entered deliberation.

"Yes, I have to tell you what my motive was and the goal I was trying to reach."

I began my defense, but Bérard, from the very first words, sensing that I had too much truth to tell and that I was going to uncover the social wounds, tried to shut me up. I kept going. Shaking of the bell, threat of expulsion. There was an uproar in the courtroom and he threatened to clear it out. Silence was restored. I kept going. After a few more words, ringing of the bell. Bérard des Glajeux was white as a sheet. He took the book and in accordance with such and such article of the law he had me thrown out by his henchmen. I had to finish by yelling out several times at the top of my lungs, "Long live the Social Revolution! Long live Anarchy!" All my fellow citizens and all my comrades joined in. Six cops took me away to the Conciergerie [prison in Paris].

Fifty thousand copies of my Defense Statement were printed and not a single one remained unsold.

# The Statement of Clément Duval

Although I don't recognize your right to question me and demand from me what you have, I've answered you as the accused.

Now, I am the accuser. I won't pretend to defend myself. What would be the point in front of people as well armed as you are, with your soldiers, guns, police, and this whole army of mercenaries who have become your guard dogs.

Let's be logical, you have the force, take advantage of it, and if you need the head of an anarchist, take it. The day of settlement will take this into account and I really hope that on that day the anarchists will measure up to their task and be pitiless, since their victims will never equal the number of yours!

I'm not talking just to you, but to all of society, that cruel mother, that selfish, corrupt society where we see orgy on one side and misery on the other!

You charge me with robbery, as if a worker who owns nothing can be a robber.

No, robbery exists only in the exploitation of man by man, in short, by those who live at the expense of the working class. It is not a robbery I committed, but a just restitution done in the name of humanity. The money was meant for revolutionary propaganda in writing and deed. It was going to be used to print newspapers and pamphlets in order to reveal the truth to the people—they've been deceived for long enough—and to show the cure to whoever feels sick.

It was going to be used for devising and building what's necessary for the day of battle, the day when the workers will wake up and snap out of their apathy and lifelessness. For it's time that this diabolical plot of the old world disappear to make way for institutions where everyone will find a more equitable lot, which exists only in anarchist communities.

Because Anarchy is the negation of all authority.

And authority is the biggest social wound because man is not free and man should be free to do whatever he wants, as long as he doesn't infringe on the freedom of his fellow men—or else he becomes a despot in turn.

In communism man contributes to society according to his abilities and his strengths; he should receive according to his needs. Men form groups and seek one another out according to their characters, abilities, and affinities, taking as a model the group that works best, rejecting vanity and stupid pride, looking only to do better than his comrade so that his comrade might do better himself.

Then we'll get useful masterpieces out of this, no more minds reduced to nothing by capital because men will be able evolve freely, no longer being under the despotic yoke of authority and individual ownership. And these groups will exchange their products with one another without restrictions.

They will learn about and feel the benefits of governing themselves and they will be federalized and make up a great family of workers all joined together for the happiness of all—one for all, all for one—recognizing only one law: the law of solidarity, of reciprocity.

No more gold, that vile metal that is the reason I am here and that I despise. Vile metal, cause of all the evils, of all the vices that afflict humanity. Vile metal with which they buy the consciences of men.

With anarchist communism no more exploitation of man by man, no more of these sweat-eaters, no more of these mercenary, predatory, selfish, poisoning shopkeepers who falsify their products and their goods and degenerate the human race. You cannot deny it because you are even forced to watch over the sellers of children's toys who poison them so young with their toys for poor, little, barely born creatures.

And those factories where they risk the workers' lives with unparalleled shamelessness, like the white lead factories where after a few months the workers become paralyzed and often die … the makers of mercury glass who quickly become bald, paralytic, have decayed bones, and die in hideous suffering!

Well, there are scientists who know that we can replace these unhealthy products with others that are harmless. Doctors who see these poor people writhing in such cruel agonies and who let this crime, this outrage against humanity, be committed. They go even further and reward the factory bosses; they bestow honorary awards on them in memory of the service they render to industry and humanity.

And how many of these unhealthy industries are there? Too many to count them all and I won't even mention the foul and unhealthy capitalist labor camps where the worker is imprisoned for ten or twelve hours a day and just to keep a little of his family's bread is forced to suffer the put-downs and humiliation of an arrogant slave driver who only needs a whip to remind us of the good old days of ancient slavery and medieval serfdom.

And those poor miners, imprisoned five or six hundred feet under ground, seeing the light of day no more than once a week and when they are exhausted by so much misery and suffering and lift up their heads to reclaim their right to the sun and to life's banquet—an army at the service of the exploiters quickly takes the field and shoots the rabble! There's plenty of proof.

And the exploitation of man by man is nothing compared to that of woman. Nature, which is so ungrateful in this respect, makes her sickly fifteen days a month, but they don't care: flesh for profit, flesh for pleasure—that's the fate of woman. So many young girls coming from the country, strong and healthy, whom they imprison in workshops, rooms only big enough for four and there are fifteen or twenty of them squeezed in, so they don't have enough air to breathe—only foul air. And with the hardships they're forced to suffer, they're anemic after six months. These poor women become sick, weak, and disgusted with work that doesn't fulfill their needs and then they are led to prostitution.

What does society do for these victims? It throws them out like lepers, registers their names, recruits them into the police, and makes them inform on their lovers.

And do you think that a worker with unselfish, noble sentiments can see this picture of human life constantly unroll before his eyes without revolting against it? He who feels all its effects and who is constantly its victim, morally, physically, and materially; he whom they take at twenty years old to pay the blood tax, to use his flesh against bullets to defend the properties and privileges of his masters; and he comes back from this slaughter crippled by it or with a sickness that makes him half-disabled, that makes him roll from hospital to hospital, using his flesh for the experiments of the Gentlemen of Science. I know what I'm talking about: I came back from this carnage with two wounds and rheumatism, sicknesses that have already earned me four years in the hospital and that prevent me from working six months of the year. Now, if you do not have the courage to take my head, which they want, as a reward for all this I'm going to die in a penal colony.

And these crimes are committed in broad daylight after having been plotted in office corridors under the influence of an inner circle or at the caprice of a woman, shouting above the rooftops: the People are sovereign, the Nation sovereign; and with the backing of high-flown words like Glory, Honor, and Country, as if there should be different countries here for beings all living on the same planet.

No! Anarchists have only one country—it is humanity.

It is also in the name of civilization that they make these expeditions abroad where thousands of men are killed with bloodthirsty savagery. It is in the name of civilization that they burn, pillage, and massacre an entire people who only ask to live in peace with them. And these crimes are committed with impunity because the penal code doesn't apply to this kind of theft, to these kinds of armed robberies. On the contrary, they give honors to those who have successfully pulled off all the carnage and medals to the mercenaries who have taken part in it, to thank them for their noble actions;

and these unthinking men are proud to wear this badge that is nothing but a certificate of murder.

But on the other hand the code severely punishes the worker to whom society refuses the right to survival and who has the courage to take what he needs (but does not have) where there is excess. Ah! Then they treat him like a thief, they arraign him in the courts and exile him to a penal colony until the end his days.

That's the logic of the present society.

Well, it's for this crime that I am here: for not recognizing these people's right to die of excess while the producers, the creators of all the social wealth die of hunger. Yes, I am the enemy of individual property and a long time ago I agreed with Proudhon that property is theft.

In fact, how do they get property if not by stealing, by exploiting their fellow men, by giving three francs to the exploited for work that will return ten to the exploiter? And the small exploiters are no better than the big ones. A proof: I saw my companion do some work, two little separate pieces of lace trimming, perfect finishing work—as a subcontracted worker she was paid seven and a half cents a piece. Fifteen days later, doing the same work as an employee, they paid her fifty-five cents apiece.

So, do you think that a mindful worker could be so stupid, on the day the rent is due, as to give back to the exploiter-owner part of the salary that had just been given to him? And he will see his wife and children forced to go without the necessities of life while that idler with this money will go to the Stock Market or somewhere else to speculate and gamble on the people's misery, or to some fashionable boudoir to wallow in the arms of a poor girl who, in order to live, is forced to turn her flesh into a pleasure toy despite being disgusted by these dogs.

Well, because I don't want to become an accomplice of such sordidness I won't pay the rent (which you reproach me for), because I don't want to let myself be robbed by that thief, that vulture they call the owner. And that's why they've given me bad references in the different places I've lived. They don't give good references except for despicable, groveling people who have no backbone. Since the law is the accomplice of owners in everything, they cast anathema on the workers who proudly lift up their heads and preserve their dignity by revolting against the abuses, injustices, and monsters like that who make up the society of owners.

And I have relied only on my conscience for a long time, scoffing at mean and stupid people, but being sure to earn the respect of the good-hearted men who have known me personally. That's why I say to you: when you condemn me you are not condemning a thief, but a mindful worker who doesn't consider himself a beast of burden to be taxed at your mercy and who recognizes the undeniable right that nature gives to every human being: the right to exist. And when society refuses this right, you have to grab it and not give it a hand. It's cowardice in a society where everything is overflowing, where everything is in abundance, which should be a source of well-being, but is now only a source of miseries ... Why? Because everything is monopolized by a handful of idle rich whose bellies are bursting while the workers are constantly in search of breadcrumbs.

No! I do not rob, I have been robbed. I am a righter of wrongs who says that all things are for all people and it's because of this strict logic of the anarchist idea that your knees are shaking.

No, I am not a thief. I am a genuine revolutionary with the courage of my convictions and devoted to the cause.

In today's society, since money is the sinews of war, I would have done everything in my power to get some and serve this cause that is so just and noble and that must free humanity from all the tyrannies and persecutions it suffers so cruelly.

Ah! I have only one regret—it is to have fallen so early into your hands. And therefore I have been prevented from satisfying an implacable hatred and a thirst for vengeance that I have for such a revolting society.

But I am comforted by the fact that some fighters remain on the go because despite all the persecutions the anarchist idea has taken seed and the theoretical development has ended and will soon make way for the practical, for action. Oh! On that day, rotten society, government, judges, exploiters of every kind, *you will have seen your day.*

*Long live the social revolution! Long live anarchy …*

❊  ❊  ❊

They obviously did not like these few truths I had to say and after two previous threats of expulsion they threw out the audience by force at 4:30 and they arrested my companion and some comrades who were all released at 9:00 that night … At 7:30 they took me out of my cell to bring me to the clerk's office of the Conciergerie where the clerk of the court read to me the verdict of those skirts and their sidekicks: "Sentenced to death."

The clerk was allowed a comment and made this remark on my attitude: his role was over, he had nothing to add, and his attitude was as he liked (whatever that was). Then he said that I laughed at the verdict since I didn't recognize men's right to judge other men because to judge a man you have to be that man and feel what he feels.

They put the straitjacket on me (without tightening it) and then two officers sent from police headquarters waited—they locked them in with me in one of the special cells for those sentenced to death.

The sergeant of the Conciergerie was very polite and accommodating. When I told him I needed to eat, even though it was late he got some food and a quarter liter of wine for me from the outside. The two officers were also very decent. They made some tactful comments and because I was overexcited by the day, I propagandized them until two in the morning.

After Madam Lemaire, the plaintiff, was questioned, she asked the presiding judge Bérard des Glajeux if it was necessary for her to show up the next day at the proceedings. When the answer was negative, Mister Labori saw a very serious error in procedure and told me, "It's absolutely necessary to lodge an appeal."

When I objected that it was acknowledging the judge's right to pronounce a sentence, he answered, "The ruling will certainly be nullified and we will go to another court. Since you're an anarchist and you want to propagate your ideas, it's a good way!"

Not wanting to miss the opportunity, I applied for an appeal, but in vain. The ruling was not nullified.

The next day, I was transferred to La Roquette prison. When I got there, they switched the old straitjacket for a new one (which they tightened up this time) along with the prison suit, toiletries, close-cropped haircut, and my beard completely shaved off.

Then we went up some stairs and down a long corridor at the end of which we went down some more stairs and I was surprised to see sunlight again in an arcade below the infirmary and music building. In La Roquette language the music building is where they isolate informers fearing that out among their comrades whom they betrayed, the latter would give them a well-deserved thrashing (for in all cases, a traitor is always a traitor and a snitch is always a snitch. But later I met some of these momentary traitors who were good men and regretted what they had done through lack of experience and under the influence of crafty and shameless judges).

Then we went into the courtyard where there is the large entry door of the death row cells. There are three of them, two pretty big ones and a third smaller one in between. I took my place in the left one with two policemen and a prison guard. The guard was relieved every two hours; the officers were on duty from six in the morning to six in the evening, two others replacing them during the night. There were six of them to take care of this service, with meals, and earning one franc more a day. That's how I figured out the daily cost of someone sentenced to death. Six officers at the rate of six francs a day, thirty-six francs; an extra guard, four francs; heat, lighting, bedding, food, three francs. Total, forty-three francs.

The warden, named Beauquesne, came to see me. After he talked to me and gave me his advice—be calm, etc.—I responded that his behavior toward me, as well as that of the officers in charge of guarding me, would dictate mine.

At 2:00 my companion came to see me. They came into my cell and took off my straitjacket, which they did not put back on, I guess to keep it out of sight of my companion who came to see me every day.

On February 23, at 8:00 p.m., the warden, followed by his staff of jailors, came to tell me of my commutation of sentence. He sent back the officers and they brought me up to the music building where I stayed until March 1. It was then that I saw that there were not only informers, but also rebellious types there who were not willing to bend to certain articles of regulation that they found too arbitrary. I got a welcome from them that I will always remember intensely.

Moreover, I have no bad feelings about this prison. The warden was always polite and my guards were reasonable, except for the sergeant who made me send him walking because of his petty annoyance about the chaplain whom he wanted me to ask to come see me in my cell. And there was an officer who wanted me to go to mass so he could go to the chapel. I laughed in his face saying that he must be joking because his malice was glaringly obvious.

On March 1 I got back in the paddy wagon along with two police officers and two on horseback escorting the wagon and bound for the Court of Appeals where I saw men no longer dressed in red but in green, who informed me that since the good bourgeoisie did not have the courage to carry out their death sentence I was sentenced to hard labor for life.

# Chapter 2
# The Healthiest Penitentiary in Guiana

I liked young [Louis Alphonse] Austruy. I liked his Parisian mischievousness and the answers he gave the medicine men to their questions and stupid comments about the act that got him condemned to death and remitted to a life sentence. I liked him even more when he told me about the act that got him sentenced to death, the act of a righter of wrongs. He was in Clairvaux [prison in Lyon], doing ten years there, and the guard posted in his wing liked to torment him. Every day brought new humiliations: arbitrary rules, false reports, etc., each time earning him a trip to the disciplinary court. One day Austruy asked the guard why he was giving him such a hard time and if he was going to stop anytime soon.

"Ah! It's not going to stop. You'll see a lot more, maggot, I'll make you die in the hole."

From that day on Austruy was resigned to his fate and to his executioner's intentions. So he prepared a little canvas bag and when he took his walk he filled it with sand and waited for a new provocation from his persecutor, who did not make him wait long; and it was not his lucky day. Austruy is a really big guy and he smacked the guard on the neck with his bag so hard that it took his breath away—his last breath. Justice was served to the wretch.

There was a revolution among the slave drivers in the prison: all of them rushed upon the righter of wrongs and beat him with their clubs and keys. They brought him to the hole more dead than alive. In the trial he explained the motives that had compelled him to act and he took full responsibility for it. He was sentenced to death. According to what he told me, it was then that the good comrade [Peter] Kropotkine, always ready to defend the weak and oppressed, and who was at that time being held in Clairvaux after the unjust trial in Lyon [1883–86], made an inquiry, got involved in the case and saved his life. I can tell you that Austruy was not ungrateful. Many times he showed his gratitude to the old fighter, which often reflected back on me, his comrade in Gehenna. When he found out that I was an anarchist he trusted me completely, told me about his plans, etc. Seeing that he was a good guy, I did my best to make him an adept. I could not succeed; he was too unpredictable and wild. All the hardships suffered at his young age were bound to make him go bad in such an environment.

❊ ❊ ❊

If they had told me I was going to spend so many years in the Salvation Islands, I would certainly not have believed them. From the first day I thought that it was the last for me, as well as for Austruy and [Jules Désiré] Marquant, when we saw the way the landing was managed.

On one of the crossbeams of a big iron barge stood the guard Patrona, the transport boss. On another crossbeam was another slave driver whose name I forget. Between them a fight broke out about who could hold the record for the crudest insults thrown at the convicts, whom they piled up helter-skelter on the barge. Whoever did not board fast enough they pushed so violently that they fell onto their comrades in front of them. And each time there was a "Hurrah!" of mad laughter from all the slave drivers, their wives, the crew, etc.

We were pale with anger and rage at our powerlessness to stop such a spectacle, but the cowardice of the convicts disgusted us even more. It was agreed among Austruy, Marquant, and I that if one of us were shoved or insulted by any of the slave drivers on the crossbeams of the barge, we would throw them into the sea (it was an easy thing to do and the only thing we could do) and jump in with them.

We were lucky to be agile enough to avoid the shoving and the insults, which kept us from acting. The landing on Saint Joseph Island went like that for us without a hitch. It was not the same for everyone, but no one protested, not a word from these reputedly dangerous men, who were actually sheep.

We were greeted by the guard Borde (from Lyon) and another named Gafuri, who made us line up like young soldiers. The boss guard from Royal Island, Casset, showed up: he was a cretin unlike any other and he owed his stripes to the favors his wife granted Commandant Cerveille, a fact well known to all the transport personnel. Every time the convicts could get hold of the horns of a steer, [the symbol of a cuckold], which had been slaughtered for food, they put them in front of his door to pay him their respects, which always made him furious.

Was it in this fury that he came to Saint Joseph Island? His first words were these: "Lowlife scum all of you, I'm going to take you down if you don't walk straight. The cell, the hole, the irons, and the gun will make you crumble."

Bunch of lowlifes and crooks, these were his favorite words. Marquant, Austruy, and I looked at one another: I was about to protest against using such language with us, but Marquant did not give me time. He said, "Boss guard, sir, we've been sent here to serve the sentence that was given to us by the courts and not to be insulted. Besides, regulations expressly forbid you to do this, under threat of severe punishments, even dismissal."

"I don't give a damn about regulations. The regulation is me and I'm going to start by chucking you in the hole, you agitator. What's your name?"

"Marquant."

"Guard, write down his name and number, tomorrow he's in the report! He'll have sixty days in the cell and both feet in irons. Okay, buddy, I'm going to take you down, you lowlife, you crook!"

"No more insults, I won't put up with them."

Austruy and I were about to do the same thing.

Marquant's energetic attitude had also awakened some other energetic characters who were momentarily sleeping under such circumstances, as I was able to see later. There's no doubt that if Casset had continued in that tone of voice or had them take Marquant away, a revolt would have broken out. He understood it at the time, I'm sure, because he turned pale and Marquant was not punished.

After that they made us open our bags and they began clearing out our things and took one of the two pairs of shoes we had received at Avignon before leaving; very few had any extra linen (from the mess hall by those with some money), since everything had been sold in Toulon or at Fort Lamalque, where the first to arrive stayed for more than a month, or on the Orne, and only for a few chaws of tobacco or some cigarettes.

We can say with Zola that "there are no rogues like honest men" who take advantage of another's misfortune to rob him more easily.

After that we went up to the camp and set up in the dirty, foul cabins that were swarming with spiders, crabs, centipedes, scorpions, snakes, etc. We could not believe that that was where we had to stay. They let us take some palm leaves to make brooms so that we could clean up, and we put some on the damp cobblestones and slabs also. We did not get hammocks until three weeks after we got there, and not all of us.

From every corner you could hear their thoughts: How? Since the Penitentiary was informed of our arrival by the Ministry, seeing that legislation had now been passed that those sentenced to hard labor would be dispatched to Guiana, how could they set us up like this?

Fourteen years later, when I left the Islands for Maroni, it was still pretty much the same thing. But at least the bread was better; it would even have been excellent if it had been worked properly. On our arrival the bread was inedible, made with almost completely rotten flour. It looked and tasted like it came from the siege of Paris in 1870. See, Commandant Cerveille and the stock keeper found a lovely profit to turn here. They decided to sell the good flour and to palm off the bad flour to the convoy (honest people figured it was good enough for rats like us). As for myself, I was never able to eat a piece of this bread, or so-called bread, during the five days that I stayed on Saint Joseph. A few others and I survived only by pilfering coconuts.

And not only was the bread inedible, but the bacalhau [dried cod] was rotten, the stew was rotten, the dried vegetables were rotten … and a lot of the men got sick.

Some were bitten in the night by hairy spiders, big as toads, commonly called crab spiders, whose bite can be fatal if not treated immediately. Many were stung by centipedes (the common name), including me. I noticed that the place where I was stung was painful and swollen and almost immediately I got a fever, which sometimes rose really high. After I was stung several times, I knew it right away.

There were also a ridiculous number of flies, and species of wasps and hornets whose sting gives a sharp pain and also brings on fever. Unfortunate the man on his forest-clearing chore who strikes the felled trees with his machete: he is attacked and soon has a head like a bushel, his face instantaneously swollen to the point that you can only see his eyes and he is in horrible pain. I once had the pleasure of getting to know these charming little beasts.

We hunted the snakes that occasionally paid us a visit, a small species called the grage snake (I do not know the name of this species) [bothrops atrox or lancehead], whose bite is one of the most venomous, and deadly. We beat the bushes around the cabins and killed a lot of them, even the biggest ones. There were a lot of grass snakes, too. Today because of the construction, the clearing of the forest and the roads built since then, the animals that were the terror of newcomers are scarcer and nothing (or little) to be scared of.

There is also a big fly called the blue fly that buzzes around a man but does not attack unless it is chased. Unfortunate the man who is stung (which never happened during my stay on the Islands). This fly is the terror of the crab spiders. It buzzes around the spider for a long time, making it listen to its buzzing glee, and then all of a sudden it dives at the spider, stings its head and kills it on the spot, goes buzzing around again and then drags the spider far away and lays its eggs. I witnessed this act that amazed Doctor Parnet, a major in the Navy, who was part of my convoy.

On the Islands there were no ticks (burrowing fleas) or mosquitoes; it was certainly the healthiest penitentiary in Guiana, the sanitarium of the sick. Free personnel and convicts alike came there from the other penitentiaries, construction sites, etc.

❊  ❊  ❊

The day after our arrival they sent us to work, scattering us into different parts to clear the forest or carry rocks from one place to another and then back again, giving each guard either fifty, or seventy-five, or ninety men accompanied by Arab or black foremen. There were no whites at that time. I was assigned with Austruy to a chore near the quay.

There we saw the transport boss Patrona come around 8:00 p.m. with six boatmen on dinghies carrying the provisions; we even lent a hand to unload them. When he had finished, Patrona drank some absinthe with his colleagues, taking away with him our chore guard named Visseau, a former soldier of the Republican Guard, a good fellow who quit in his third year because he could not commit the evils that his colleagues did.

The boatmen, for their part, went to pilfer coconuts, thus abandoning the dinghy, totally armed, at the quay. We only had to jump in, take the oars and skedaddle out of there. That's the idea that came to me right away, which I shared with Austruy and with a Breton (whose intentions I knew), an excellent seaman who had been sailing since he was young, which is why they called him Le Mousse [Cabin Boy]. They agreed with me, but they both wanted to go and get some comrades they had promised to escape with.

I told them: "Your friends will find another opportunity later on, but I'm begging you, let's not miss this one. By the time you find your comrades in their other chores, it'll be too late; in ours we can find five men who would ask nothing better than to go with us."

And I named those who wanted to escape.

"No, no, no, we're going to go get so-and-so and so-and-so!"

"Go on," I said to them, "but it's no use, it's lost …"

Indeed, they came back half an hour later with their comrades, but it was too late. Patrona and the boatmen were getting on board to return to Royal Island. They were always sorry for having missed such a wonderful opportunity that never came up again. The following day, doing the same chore, we saw them arrive with the provisions and an extra guard, who stayed in the dinghy along with the boatmen, oars in hand, while Patrona went up to camp to sip his absinthe.

The thing had leaked out and a few days later we were sent to Royal Island, along with the comrades who had been fetched. But first we were paid a visit by Commandant Cerveille, called the Wild Boar of the Ardennes, whose ferocity the convicts had composed a song about. It often happened that when someone was brought before him he insulted him, slapped him, and hit him with his cane or umbrella. I was so outraged by the cowardice of those who accepted this that I said out loud that I hoped the same thing would happen to me.

They informed us in the cabins that the Commandant wanted to see us before classifying us and so we would not be off to our chores in the morning. Before making us go out for the roll call, we saw the Commandant hit an old man with his umbrella, a guy classified among the lepers (though he was not one at all, only having the secondary or tertiary effects of syphilis). He was coming back from the kitchen looking for provisions for himself and his comrades. Since the kitchen was at the bottom of camp, it was the only way to go back up to the building that today is used as a prison, as cells, but at that time was reserved for the lepers and the crazies. Outraged and fearing that the same thing would happen to me without anything to defend myself, I went out through the back of the cabin and armed myself with a big rock that I put in my pocket. The only one who saw me was a guy named Raseneuve, but he didn't say a word: I had nothing to fear from this convict.

They called the roll and made us form a circle around the Commandant who gave us a fitting speech with all the administrative patter, to behave ourselves well, that we would be granted concessions, etc. We already knew what to expect about what they called good behavior—read "snitch," "despicable creep" … He wasn't very eloquent because of his stammering and had a lot of trouble expressing himself. When he had finished, he called up a young Corsican and congratulated him on a letter he had written to his family when he arrived. In the letter he spoke in very good terms about the Administration, the slave drivers and the Commandant in particular, saying that though his life sentence for vendetta had separated him from his family, he would find another in the military guards among whom were many of his compatriots and he would find a father in the Commandant. That put him in the good graces of the "good father." The next day he sent him to Royal Island and took him in like a houseboy. When he left he raised him up a class and sent him to another penitentiary in Cayenne with high recommendations, which made him get better work. I don't know if he knew how to make the best use of it or if he died; I never saw him again.

Having written to my companion about my arrival, I in turn was called up because of my letter, but not to receive congratulations.

"How can you, you, you, a former sol-sol-soldier, insult the military guards in this letter? You call them surveillance agents!"

"It's French. I didn't know at the time that they were called military guards. Anyway, the title shouldn't be offensive, it's perfectly good French: we say customs agents, tax agents …"

"You have insulted these good noncommissioned officers. I'm going to send your letter to the Supervisor's office; it will not be sent and you will be severely punished."

"You're in quite a hurry to commit such an injustice against me."

"Guard, take down the number of, of, of this anarchist … Ah, is it you who said that all who own things are thieves?"

"Yes, all who own things do so at the cost of those who own nothing and consequently are thieves—especially the civil servants and the establishment, who consume a lot and produce absolutely nothing."

Pale with anger, he did not know what to make of this and said to me, "Ha! You're one of those who want to burn down all of France!"

"A large part of it, yes, because, you see, only fire and dynamite can purify society of the rotten bourgeoisie."

He clearly felt that he was not having an easy job of it in front of his subordinates and the convicts. Raging mad and all the while fondling his umbrella (and I my rock) he said to me, "Cal-cal-calm down and go back to your place."

"I am very calm. You provoked me and I answered as I should."

"B-b-be quiet!"

Then he turned to the guard Borde, who acted as the camp boss, and while rattling his umbrella, "Did you ever think you'd see such stubborn mules?"

We broke ranks and we headed back to the cabin. During the entire siesta we talked about anarchy, a word that most were ignorant of.

The next day, seven of us (all who had wanted to get hold of the dinghy) went to Royal Island where they gave us hammocks right away—we were spoiled.

The day after that, under the watch of a slave driver, I went to report to the Commandant who said to me, "The works foreman needs workers of your profession, so I'm classifying you for the works. You will start in one hour."

"Excuse me, Commandant, may I say something about that?"

"You have nothing to say. You have to obey or else I will use the means that are in my power."

"Use them right away, then, because I refuse. I don't refuse to work, but to do certain work that is against my principles."

"What does that mean?"

"I will never do the work given to workers of my profession here (black-smiths, metalworkers, [locksmiths]), which most of the time consists in preparing instruments of torture and inquisition: bars of justice [steel poles that run through the manacles securing the prisoners by the ankles to their beds], shackles, repairing handcuffs, sharpening the guillotine's blade, and such. And I tell you with all sincerity that no human power will force me to do something that offends my conscience, so it's useless to insist. Leave me to the chores instead, it's preferable."

"You will go to the works."

"Okay, if you agree that I won't do what I just said."

"We'll see about that, I am the master."

"It's already seen; and even though I'm a convict I consider myself freer than you because I will never do anything but what my conscience dictates."

He started looking impatient and angry and said to the guard, "Take this stubborn mule away."

After roll call at 12:30, I marched out with the other workers and they gave me a job that had nothing inquisitorial about it. For ten days all went well. During this time I went to see the Major to ask if he would have a pair of shoes custom made for me, because my feet were deformed by the rheuma-tism contracted during the war of 1870. He gave in to the evidence and right away signed a voucher to make shoes with canvas uppers (special shoes for the crippled). But Commandant Cerveille, out of revenge, refused to sign the voucher. Without his signature, the Major's was worth nothing—they would not make the shoes. They gave the seniors clothing and I was called to get a pair of clodhoppers. Unaware of the Commandant's refusal at the time, I said to the boss guard Casset, "Don't bother, I should be getting some custom-made shoes. While I'm waiting for them, just leave me the old ones. They're way too big and that's a pain, but I need the width for my feet, whereas I'll be forced to cut the ones you're giving me."

"I don't give a damn," the brute answered, "take these shoes, it's your feet, and give me the old ones."

"If that's what you want, but I'm warning you that I'm going to have to cut them."

"I don't give a damn, I don't give a damn ..."

Seeing that it was impossible to make the cretin listen to reason, I took the shoes and gave him my old ones. It was a frame-up that came to fruition in no time.

The following day the guard in charge of my squad's roll call said to me, "You've cut your shoes."

"I had no choice. Look at my feet."

He reported it right away to Casset and the next day after roll call at noon they gave me sixty days of solitary for willful destruction of clothes belonging to the State. Before I had time to protest or even say one word, two guards led me not to the cell but to the big prison, with irons on both feet, and every day the men punished with prison or the cell went to work, except for me.

Faced with such an arbitrary punishment I thought that the Major would protest since he had certified my infirmity. (Poor fool, I should have figured that being an anarchist I was totally worthless in the eyes of all bureaucrats.) Nevertheless, my request for a medical visit was confirmed for the next day (even though they did not want to let me go) and when he saw me I told him that I wasn't sick, but that it was to get on record the abuse I was the victim of.

"The Commandant didn't want to sign the voucher, there was nothing I could do." (That's how I found out about the refusal.)

"What! You, a man of science who are the only one competent in this matter, you let them cancel out your signature like that! That's really too bad for you, sir, and I'm very sorry to have bothered you."

"It's okay," he said, staring at me, "I'll see the Commandant tomorrow."

Then he visited the prison and told the guard that it was filthy, it smelled bad, and so on, that they needed to clean the cots with boiling water and then disinfect and whitewash the walls. "Furthermore, I'm going to see the Commandant about it."

The Commandant backed him up right away.

The next day some men on chores (as a matter of form) did the said cleaning, which managed to make us devoured even more by the vermin, which were not destroyed but angry at being disturbed. The lice and the bedbugs ran around on the cots, the fleas jumped around all over the place, the scorpions stung, the centipedes bit, etc.

Two days after the Major's visit, I got one from the camp boss Casset armed with a pizzle whip [made from bull testicles], along with a prison guard. Casset informed me that my punishment was reduced to thirty days in the cell.

"I didn't ask for pity or mercy, I just reported the injustice of such a punishment, the deceitfulness, etc. I thought I'd been understood by Doctor Parnet, I realized it's nothing like that. Oh well."

This reply managed to exasperate Casset so much that he started walking around the prison shaking his pizzle and reeling off his insolent vocabulary at all the anarchists in general and me in particular, underlining every crude remark with a smile; every insult was addressed to me when he passed by.

I couldn't put up with it any longer. I was in a rage because of my powerlessness, with irons around my two feet, and I screamed at them, "Cowards, bums! To insult a man in such a situation. Come on, take off my chains! Even unarmed as I am and you with all your guns and your pizzle, you will see that a man of courage, an anarchist, is not scared of two cowards, two imps like you."

"Ha, ha, ha! My boy," Casset snickered, "tomorrow in the report those words are going to earn you ninety days in the cell, if not a court-martial, for death threats, ha, ha, ha! Good night, Mister Anarchist!"

When they left, tears ran down my cheeks and I resolved to do away with Casset the first chance I got. I was living for nothing but that; I couldn't wait to avenge such an outrage.

The punished men came back from work and seeing me so overexcited they asked me what was wrong. I told them all about Casset's visit and to a few whom I thought I could trust (not yet knowing at this time what the environment was like; unfortunately, I was bound to learn it at my own expense)

I told the decision I had made and that I couldn't wait to carry it out ... The next day, as soon as the prison opened, Casset knew what I intended to do. Ten or eleven days went by before he came back to the prison. As always I was alone during the work hours and he looked at me but did not say a word.

Two days after this silent visit [May 23 or 24, 1887], they informed six of the punished men that they would not go to work in the morning and an hour after the march they unlocked my irons, gave us our bags, and all seven of us left the prison. They made us line up with a bunch of others who were already there with their bags. Roll call was made. When I saw all these poor men with their faces shining with joy, I asked my neighbor, "Why the roll call?"

"A convoy for Cayenne. We're leaving at eleven on the Oyapock (naval dispatch boat)."

Despite all the preparations that I saw made, the distribution of wine, etc., I could not believe I was really leaving. I was afraid they would call me back any minute and tell me it was all a mistake; I was in doubt until the boat left. It was only when the anchor was lifted that I found Marquant and Austruy (they also were part of the convoy) and all three of us were happy to be sailing into the unknown with hearts full of hope. We withdrew into a corner to talk about our plans. Marquant was afraid of the sea and wanted to leave by land. Austruy and I did not agree, even though we were also sick like him during part of the crossing, which lasted five hours because the sea was very rough.

When we got to the harbor and saw the dinghies dragging around and all the boats, we figured that it was possible to get one, if, however, they were not boarded in the evening. We disembarked and crossed the town to go to the penitentiary. The whole way the inhabitants watched us open-mouthed; it had been a long time since they had seen so many whites (there were a hundred of us).

It was almost six when we got to the penitentiary. The roll call was not finished, so they made us line up. We saw the guards report the call to the camp boss and then the Arabs (there were a lot of them) marched back to their cabins. Then they made us move closer to the Europeans (there were very few of them). One of them stepped out from his squad, moved forward a few steps and took off his hat; the other convicts as well as the prison guards did the same and then they ordered us to do so also. We were very surprised to see and hear the one who had stepped out of the ranks start reciting a Pater [Noster] and an Ave [Maria]. Seeing what it was all about I put my hat back on. A guard gave me the sign to take it off again. I denied him.

After the prayer he went to find the camp boss and asked him if he had to make a report for disobedience. The chief prison guard smiled and said that he supported freedom of conscience.

Following that they made us break ranks with the veterans and they led us rookies to a cabin where we set up our hammocks. At this time all the cabins were open. We went to see the veterans and we walked with them around the camp until 7:30 in the evening, the time to go to bed. They were glad we had come and showed it; for a long time they had suffered the yoke of the Arabs who far outnumbered them and continually showed their hatred of the Roumi [Christians]. Every day there were bloody battles, which greatly pleased the slave drivers and all the personnel of the administration.

It did not take us long to learn the truth of what we were told by the veterans. At 8:00 p.m. (the time to be quiet), the Arab foremen came into our cabins armed with matraques (big truncheons) and threatened to beat us if we made a sound.

We were firmly resolved not to let ourselves be bullied by this gang of brutes, so we stood up to some of them and said that we would sort it all out when it was day and they should not think they could do what they usually did. Since we got there on Saturday and Sunday was a day off, after roll call we debriefed our friends on the visit and on the threat of the Arab foremen and on what we planned to do about it if they made the slightest move on us, and while we were talking about it everyone should figure out what he could do. All of a sudden an avalanche of foremen (along with a guard) spread throughout the camp. They were ordered to gather us up to make us change cabins, which did not happen without insults and threats on both sides. They made the Arabs move and we took their place, doing the necessary cleaning of the dirty, disgusting cabin they had just left. Some foremen helped us and congratulated us; they were the least rude.

When the cleaning was done and we were set up, some of us left to walk around the camp and others with tears in their eyes put away their precious little belongings that reminded them of their lost loved ones. There were around fifty of us in the cabin. Marquant, Austruy, and I and seven or eight others, whose names I don't recall, talked about our present situation and how to escape from it, because it was not smiling on any of us.

One of us had to go to the toilet and he met a foreman on the stairs who asked him pretty rudely to do a chore in the camp. Our comrade answered that he did not obey the orders of a convict like himself and he kept going down the stairs. Not used to being refused, the slave drivers' flunky got furious and wanted to bludgeon the guy who dared to do such a thing. He halfway prepared the blow, but another foreman below kicked him in the butt. Our comrade came back up fast, pushed the foreman down the stairs, and told us what just happened. There was a hullabaloo. Our small band knew that if we wanted to make them respect us we had to act in solidarity.

So Marquant proposed that we not let any foreman enter our cabin. The proposition was unanimously accepted and the opportunity to put it into effect was not long in coming.

A foreman came to see what was happening in our cabin. As soon as we saw him we asked him to leave. After we refused to let him in he threatened us, so we forced him down the stairs faster than he had come up!

He came back with eight of his colleagues. During this time we prepared our defense: we dismantled our hammocks and put the sticks at arm's reach in case we needed them.

When they came to the top of the stairs, we asked them to leave like we did to the first. Seeing our attitude, some of them wanted to talk it out, others to fight it out—and that's what happened. One of them, a solid guy, hit me hard. Before I had time to pay him back he was grabbed by one of ours, a guy called Fat Pierre who was endowed with the strength of Hercules, and thrown to the bottom of the stairwell. He was knocked almost completely senseless; blood was flowing everywhere.

We rushed to get our sticks from the hammocks and a free-for-all followed. Two foremen were thrown through the windows and two others were lying on the cabin floor unable to move an inch; the others ran away to report to the Internal Service what had just happened.

Maybe fifteen guards came running, guns in hand. A dozen stayed below and the others invaded the cabin. Among them was Guidi, the guard of first class, our convoy boss. Each of us held our ground. Austruy and I were near the stairs, so we were the first to welcome the visitors. As soon as Guidi saw me, he jumped at me and leveled his gun at my nose telling me that I was the leader of everything that was happening. It was not the time to talk, so I took his gun with one hand, put the other around his throat, and lay his head on my hammock, in complete control. At least that is what I was told by those who witnessed it, since I did not remember this detail. They also told me that in his hurry he must have forgotten to load his gun, if, however, it had ever been unloaded, because he was holding a few bullets in his left hand.

Not a shot was fired; it was the order of the boss guard who came up a minute later with the foremen who had fled so that they could point out who had taken part in the plot. Thirty-five or forty cowards who were witnesses to it, who would have very well let us be bludgeoned if we had been weaker, were also congratulated by all the slave drivers. They made no mistakes. Only one was not named: Marquant.

They led us to the cells and the wounded to the infirmary. During the day the boss guard made an investigation. Marquant asked to be heard by him if he wanted to know the exact truth: he recounted the insolence and brutality of the foremen and he stuck up for us in our act of rebellion, saying that he himself would not have put up with any attack on his dignity ... also saying that as a soldier he had been in Africa and he was familiar with the character, temperament and customs of the Arabs and their hatred for the Roumi. He said that since the administration, the guards and most of the former officers had taken their leave in Africa, they were not unaware of this and so consequently it was the administration that should assume responsibility for what had just happened, especially if he, the camp boss, did not want the same thing to happen again, and maybe worse because out of the hundred of us new arrivals more than two-thirds were serving life sentences. So, for the existence awaiting us, many of us did not care about our skin and were ready to sacrifice it to maintain our human dignity under these convict's clothes.

"So, disarm your foremen of their matraques that they use to bludgeon a lot of our comrades in misfortune who are older than us, abusing their greater number, and advise them to be less insolent and rude, etc. Then you will have calm in your camp. They did not send us here to cause disorder and that is not what any of us wants."

"After what I was told by the guard Guidi, the chief of your convoy, it's maybe not the same with one of your colleagues, Duval, the anarchist, who seemed to behave pretty badly on board. He wanted to be stubborn and had to be put in the hole."

"They've misled you," said Marquant and he told him what happened.

"If that's the case, it's arbitrary."

"Absolutely," said Marquant, "like you holding my comrades in cells for a longer time when they do nothing but defend themselves."

"Okay, Marquant! I'm going to take your deposition into account, continue the investigation, and question those involved."

With this in mind they sent the guard of the Internal Service to interrogate us in turn about what happened and whom I told pretty much the same story as Marquant. He was very polite in his questions and in the few remarks he made to our answers. At 4:00 p.m., the camp boss gave the order to release those who had taken part in the morning's rebellion. I was the only exception: they had consulted the file and noticed that I still had a dozen days left in my thirty-day punishment in the cell.

When those released went back to the camp they were greeted with a truly sincere ovation by the veterans and they had the pleasure of seeing the foremen without their matraques and acting a little more politely.

This proves once again that everywhere, in any situation whatsoever, you must oppose force with force to overcome anything.

# Chapter 3
# You Can Have My Fat, But Not My Skin

I spent sixteen days in prison. Since the cutter was about to sail for [Saint-Laurent-du] Maroni but was putting in at the Salvation Islands first, I got on board again, with two sick men, a European and an Arab Jew named Parianti. All three of us were being watched by the guard Visseau. The boss guard of the cutter ordered me to be put in irons, saying, "Ha! Buddy, you want to take hold of my ship, you anarchist rat, I know you."

"Don't be rude and don't use 'tu', [the informal 'you']. I won't put up with anything from a wretch like you who drowned three men after putting them in irons."

That happened around the end of 1885 or the beginning of 1886. Three deportees from the penitentiary in Maroni or Kourou, I don't remember very well, were sent to Cayenne on board the cutter to be court-martialed. They had irons put around both feet and despite the fact that the sea was rough they did not unchain them. There were lots of laughs from the captain, the crew and the guard who was with them every time the poor men were flooded by the waves.

As the sea became heavier and heavier, knowing they could be dragged off, the prisoners asked to be unchained. They laughed in their faces, treating them like cowards, saying that since they had wanted to escape it was good for them to get used to bad weather, maybe it would discourage them from starting up again, etc. (This was the story of one of the crew members, a freed convict, hired by the administration as a sailor who did not have the courage to tell the truth when he was called as a witness for the Captain when he went before the Council and was acquitted and went back to work. It was only later, when he no longer belonged to the administration that he told the truth.) One very strong wave swept them off the bridge. They fell into the sea and under such conditions there was no way to help them.

Furious at this reply, he yelled at the top of his lungs, "To the bars of justice!" The guard Visseau objected.

"I am the master on my ship."

"Absolutely," Visseau said, "but I am responsible for this deportee and I don't want the thing he's complaining about to happen again."

"It's not true, it's slander, defamation, and you believe it?"

"I hope for your sake it's slander."

"I'm going to enter this maggot into my report according to regulations."

"No insults, I won't put up with them against those who are under my watch any more than against myself. Make a report if you want to. I'll do the same and I think you won't have an easy time of it. Believe me, let it go. You don't have to worry about Duval taking your boat from you all by himself. So, there's no reason to put him in irons."

"In fact, you're right, but you know, I narrowly escaped the other time coming from the Islands. They would have chucked me in the sea, the crooks."

"I don't think so. I think they're smarter than that. They would have treated you well to put your navigating skills to good use until they were in a safe haven. You would have returned peacefully with your crew and today you would have the first class stripes that you want so badly. Hey, Duval, isn't that the way you would do it?"

I smiled but did not say a word.

The weather was beautiful, the captain was cheerful and the sailors as well. On the way they had a bite to eat and offered us some. My two travel companions, too sick to take anything in, refused, and me too, for a different reason. But I accepted from the guard Visseau, with whom I chatted for a long time during the journey, when he offered me some of the food and drink he had brought. That made the captain say that I was spiteful since I had not accepted what he had offered.

"Not at all," I said, and I always will say what I think. "It's nothing personal. You're the result of your environment, upbringing, and education, especially in the barracks or on the ships, etc."

When we got to the Islands, the guard Visseau brought us up to the Internal Service (Royal Island). Casset asked why I was coming back.

"I don't know the reason."

He sent the sick to the infirmary and told me to go to the third squad. All went well for a few days while I was working at clearing the forest.

❊   ❊   ❊

At this time there was no work on Saturday afternoon, this half-day was reserved for washing up and doing the laundry since we needed to be clean for the inspection that took place on Sunday morning—whoever was not clean got punished.

Around 3:00 p.m. I went to get shaved in the second squad where the barber was located and then I went to the water tank to get a pail of water to wash my face. While on my way over there I met the third class guard Bartholi, one of Casset's favorites. I knew that he was working at the signal station (although he barely knew how to read or write: a deportee named Brabançon, a former notary, was giving him lessons), so I was a little surprised to find him in the camp where he was never on duty during the day.

Coming back up from the water tank, the Arab Parianti, who had come with me from Cayenne, was standing there by the little infirmary situated near this place (and called the leper's infirmary). As soon as he saw me, he called me over to ask me for a paper to roll a cigarette. I gave him a few. When he left, Bartholi came over and asked me for my name and number.

"Why?" I asked him.

"It's okay, it's okay, you'll find out tomorrow."

"My name you already know. As for my number, it's printed clearly enough on my jacket."

After he left, I racked my brain trying to figure out what had led him to ask me this. Finding nothing, I knew no good could come from it, from Casset, and my resentment for him grew. For a while I had abandoned the desire to avenge the outrage he had committed against me in the hope of having the opportunity to regain my freedom soon. I told myself that, after all, there was no shortage of Cassets so it was useless to sacrifice myself for one; it would be better to do it for a few.

On Sunday there was no report, but on Monday at 12:30 roll call they announced the punishments: I was very surprised when they gave me sixty days in the cell for gambling. It was so unexpected that for a minute I sat there stunned and then I protested against the dishonesty of such a report—that firstly I was not a gambler and then that I had no money so it would be hard for me and if I had any it would be to get the necessities that I lacked because you are starving us, etc.

Since Casset had decided not to come to the roll call, it was the Captain of Arms of the first class who took it and made the line-ups for different chores. My protest in front of the convicts was not to his liking and he yelled to the guards, "Take him away!" Four of the brutes jumped on me: Rigaut, a guard of the second class, Tixier or Texier, the same, Bartholi, a guard of the third class, who had made the report, and I do not remember the fourth.

You have to be in the same situation to know what I felt: I thought I'd gone mad and I yelled, "Don't touch me, you bunch of murderers, kill me right now. The bourgeoisie didn't do it because they knew there were mercenaries here who would do the job for them. Go on! Fire, you bunch of cowards," and I tore open my jacket and bared my chest.

These words made quite an impression on all the convicts and prison guards, which I did not realize at the time because I was so overexcited. They holstered their guns and one of them, Tixier or Texier, said to me, "Come on, Duval, come with me." This Tixier or Texier was a pusher, paying well for the work that he made the convicts do illegally. But on duty he was a brute personified for whom the word "humanity" did not exist.

He put me back in the hands of the guard Haumon (an unstable fellow), who was in charge of the prisons. I was unchained all day long, walking around in my cell, except for one hour every morning in the corridor. I was the only one in solitary not going to work, no doubt with the idea that the lack of air and exercise would make me sick and that leaving me alone I would soon be done for. They were wrong. The idea of revenge, and such, haunted me constantly and in order not to lose my strength I devoted myself to physical exercise every day. At 5:00 they put the irons on only one foot. I had a good sleep from 7:00 or 8:00 p.m. until 3:00 or 4:00 in the morning and I was in good shape every day.

At the end of thirty days Haumon said to me, "You're lucky, you are, for a newcomer to the colony, you're never sick."

"I don't have to be and I'm telling you I'm not going to be. Unlike so many others, I don't want to spend my time in the hospital. You can have my fat, maybe, but not my skin. I won't be giving it to you so cheaply."

"We don't want to hurt you. Don't make us punish you."

"Ha! Be quiet and leave me alone ..."

❖   ❖   ❖

On Royal Island there is the coal depot (I think there was one in Cayenne, too) where the dispatch boat and the small steamers doing coastal trade come to stock up. When the Antillean cruiser is cruising in the waters, which rarely happens, it also gets its coal there. So, from time to time a three-master coaler comes to fill up the stock (before leaving the Islands I noticed that there was very little coal in the depot). The ship's captain, wanting his boat to be unloaded as quickly as possible, takes some convicts on loan from the administration, paying, I think, two francs a day for each of them.

So, for this he speaks to the Commandant of the penitentiary and they have a bash. After dinner, between the pear brandy and the cheese the latter says, "You want this to go quickly, we'll count fifteen men on loan and I'll give you forty or fifty of them if need be. There are a lot of them in solitary who can't go to work, so I'll give you them first and you arrange it with the transport boss. There are plenty of barges, the boys will get rid of them for you in no time."

"It's a deal," the captain says every time. "We'll arrange it once the unloading is finished." (Between honest folk things are always arranged.)

"Good, good," says the Commandant, knowing that he will get even more for the ballast of the boat, and the transport boss too if, that is, the kickback is not wanting.

The ballast is made with rocks that they take from all over the Islands, so, unfortunate the captain who does not prove generous enough to the honest civil servants. They leave him only the men assigned to the chore and they do not work them too hard. On the other hand, if the captain proves generous, they supply him with as many men as he wants and just as for the coal they give not a moment of rest to the men on this chore and the lovely slave driver's vocabulary is in full swing: "Come on, you lazy slugs, rotten, filthy, lowlife rats, etc., hurry up or I'll blow your face off!"

At this chore there are two or three slave drivers for whom the captain, a smart guy, often pours big glassfuls of absinthe and tafia, and such. However, there are sometimes guards less brutish who say to the captain, "You know, if you want the work to go fast, you have to encourage the men. It's hard work. Give them something to drink, a piece of bread, or a biscuit, or a bag of tobacco and you'll see how they'll take this stuff off. You won't have to boss them around."

They were right because every time I saw them treat these poor men decently, I saw them get everything they wanted from them, even from the most recalcitrant.

On a rest day, Sunday or a holiday, a respected guard entered the cabin asking for volunteers for such a chore, everyone stood up together like a single man. "But," the guard said, "I only need ten or fifteen men." He was often forced to choose for himself in order to avoid a ruckus. See, when it was a mean, brutal slave driver it was the opposite—he was forced to use threats to get the men he needed.

So, I was in a cell when a coaler arrived and for ten days they carried out its unloading. I was not at all surprised when one morning, a Tuesday, the guard Haumon took me and the others in solitary for this chore. I worked on it for two days, enough to become completely black. And on Thursday morning, seeing that I was not going to go to work, I asked the slave driver the reason why.

"It's finished for you."

"So, let me clean myself up and wash my clothes," etc.

"Okay, okay, you'll wash your clothes on Saturday with the others."

The Commandant and the camp boss came into the disciplinary quarters on Friday morning and asked the slave driver how I got so dirty and why he did not make me wash my clothes.

"He worked at the coal chore for two days. I tried to make him wash his clothes, but he said he would wash them on Saturday with the others."

"Oh yes!" said Commandant Cerveille. "It's so he can talk with the others, okay, you will report him for uncleanliness."

I was so stunned by such dishonesty that I could find nothing to say. The following day I was given a fifteen-day extension in the cell for uncleanliness, but not without telling the slave driver Haumon what I thought about his disgraceful conduct, about such a base act and such cold-heartedness, pronouncing my words carefully so that he would not miss a single one. He was surprised at such apparent and ironic calm and listened to me all the way to the end of the proof that I gave him of his ignoble occupation as a slave driver. He apologized and almost asked forgiveness, which I would not have given him at the time.

I finished my seventy-five days of solitary under his watch. I had nothing more to complain about from him. On the contrary, he gave me free rein (for the situation, of course) to smoke, talk with my neighbors, wash myself, etc. He was relieved a short time after I left and was used in the chores.

One day he was leading a convoy of men dragging along the handcart to bring up the materials to the camp. Since two men were enough when they went downhill, the others walked behind. An Arab somehow managed to lag a little far behind and went into the medical officer's garden near the amphitheater, in order to get some guavas to sate his hunger. Haumon saw him, shot at him twice and he hit him once in the left arm. They carried him to the hospital and despite their treatment he was crippled in that arm, which did not prevent them from punishing him with sixty days in the cell for stealing … and for what? A few rotten guavas, ha!

Haumon went before the Council, was acquitted, even got congratulated for his act of bravery, but did not return to the Islands.

❖    ❖    ❖

Commandant Cerveille was about to leave us, so a digression is necessary.

When my convoy arrived in the Islands, Commandant Cerveille had just been court-martialed for mistreatments inflicted on the convicts and this was based on the report of doctors and a Captain of Troops on Royal Island.

Here are the facts: On the East Plateau there was a cell area that was condemned by the doctors of the Island and it was prohibited to put men there because of the lack of air caused by the metal grills, shuttered doors, etc. and the humidity.

Cerveille took no account of it and kept imprisoning men in the place. They fell gravely ill and many died. A new prohibition by the doctors. So, they had to take out those who were still there and put them in the camp's big prison where they were chained by both feet night and day, exposed at every minute to the insults and humiliation of the slave drivers who made a report on the slightest pretext. Extensions were tacked on like that and they ended up doing seven or eight months in solitary for a punishment of only ninety days.

As their complaints were hushed up, they decided to put an end to these moral and physical tortures. One night they bent the bars of justice and defended themselves. Great panic throughout the camp, all the slave drivers were on their feet. The Captain and his fifty soldiers rushed into the prison. Cerveille commanded them to fire on the outlaws, who were unchained in order to escape, and murder the honest men. The Captain responded that he had been called to put down a revolt and that he would have nothing to do with this. "Simply men who didn't want to put up with your mistreatments anymore, Commandant Cerveille, and be assured that I will make a report accordingly. Soldiers, sheath your bayonets!" And, to the slave drivers: "Not one of you will touch these men."

The next day they were all admitted to the hospital (they needed it; they were all anemic) and the medical officers added their reports to the Captain's and they were all sent to the governor.

The Captain and the officers had been told about things by one of the tortured prisoners, named Garnier, a convicted soldier who was later killed in the Saint Joseph affair by the guard Mosca outside the cabin.

Commandant Cerveille, for his part, made a report against his victims that ended up with them being court-martialed, but they were all acquitted when they revealed the atrocities and infamies committed by Cerveille and his henchmen. They arraigned him, too, in order to answer the accusations. He ignored it the first and second time. The third time they sent a patrol and two gendarmes to bring him there by hook or by crook. This time he came, was hit hard by the medical officers, the Captain and the Court and got the blame that he deserved. Then he was arrested there. But he deserved more, the scoundrel—he deserved to take the place of his victims.

Nothing of the sort happened. He resumed his position and continued his despotism, inquisition and everything else for more than fifteen months after the incident. It was only on March 11, 1888, that he handed over the command to Commandant [Henri] Cor, an old drunkard and bureau chief in the administration. Cerveille was a protégé of the Ministry of the Colonies where his son was employed and he was going to enjoy a nice pension that the taxpayers prepared for him for having committed such horrors at the price of so many victims and that earned him the nickname the Wild Boar of the Ardennes.

❀   ❀   ❀

On my exit from the cell they put me back to work where I was peaceful for a little while. During this time I prepared an escape with Austruy (in desperation on a raft). We were betrayed. Material proof was lacking so we only got fifteen days in the cell.

We had done seven days when on Cerveille's order, since space was lacking in the camp, those of us doing time in solitary were transferred at 6:00 to the cells in the East, despite the express prohibition of the doctors and the reprimand of the Council. Five days after our arrival in this place, on a Saturday, they unchained us so we could do our laundry (because we were chained by a foot day and night; it was in this position that we constantly received the visits of the little snakes called pit vipers, which scared us and prevented us from sleeping. One of us, while taking a nap during the day, felt one of these reptiles slithering across his face and chest, which was completely bare because of the heat and lack of air. Luckily he had enough composure not to budge an inch and got off with just a fright).

As soon as we were unchained, after we got some air in the corridor, all of us, feeling dizzy, fell to the ground. Three days later our punishment was over and Austruy and I right away fell down outside at the feet of the foreman who had come to bring us to the Internal Service and return us to our squads.

In September 1887 the *Orne* came back again to fill up the void left by the dead from the last convoy.

At this time, until the new regulation (*Vérignon*), the cabins were open and for each there was a man in front to stand guard in two-hour shifts or pay twenty centimes to a partner to stand guard for him, in order to prevent escapes, etc., thus making the men squeal on each other. See, the man on guard was responsible for everything that happened in the cabin during his watch. He lit up his round, went by everyone's hammock and had to report anything that looked out of the ordinary. (Strange way to elevate human dignity.)

In this convoy there were a good number of Parisians who knew Austruy and who, like him, loved their freedom, and he was assailed with demands for information on how to "pair up" (Parisian slang for escape). A hoped-for chance presented itself to them. They made them clear away from the baths the large rocks that the waves had knocked down. For this they had set up a hoist. Right away the Parisians figured that if it stayed there at night, it would make an excellent raft.

They let Austruy in on it. "They won't notice we've left until morning, being all packed into the barn like we are, the rounds can't count us. There's only you because you have to come with us and how will you manage to go unnoticed until morning?"

"Wait, I'm going to talk to Duval. I don't want to leave without him."

So, he made me part of his comrades' project and I told him that they shouldn't make the mistake of trying to leave with the hoist such as it was, without floaters, since it was the hard wood of the Island and therefore not buoyant, except for a few crossbeams that had been repaired and replaced with fir. Great disappointment when he told them the news. What to do? There were barrels in the yard for rolling water. It was agreed that they would take them and I would be in on it.

Austruy and I set our sights on the barrels that we had to take, the best and nicest we could get our hands on, and waited for the day of the favorable tide. When the day arrived, it was agreed that since there were eight of us, four would go down at nightfall carrying all of our things and untie the cords of the hoist to attach the floaters, and two would come with Austruy and me to get the barrels.

Things went beautifully until a little incident happened to me while rolling a barrel. While I was going by the foremen's barracks (which later became the washhouse of the personnel), I stepped too far on the side of the embankment and fell into a hole that was used as a cesspool for these hideous characters. When I arrived at the meeting point on the seashore, I washed myself off as well as I could, but I still reeked of its stench.

All this took time and the silence had been broken for a while (it was the dark of night and we did the best we could under the circumstances). We told our comrades to prepare everything, that we had to go back up for the first round and that we would come back down right after. It was time. The man on guard (a former escapee caught in France several years back and after a few more attempts he ended up in the Islands. I don't remember his name—it's coming back to me ... Portal—but I was glad to hear one day, in 1891 I think, that he died as a leper on Devil's Island)—so, he had found out about our absence. We barely had time to get back in our hammocks when the round was made.

"Austruy, Duval," said one of the guards of the first class whose name I forget, a kind and polite man, "where have you been?"

"We were taking a newcomer back to his cabin, he couldn't see clearly."

"Good answer, but you know, I can't help it, we know your plans, boys. I don't want to hurt you for this, but watch out! I know how to do my duty if you're caught."

During this time the guard of the third class who was with him had not whispered a word. All of a sudden he said, "Goddamn it ... it smells like sh— in here."

Austruy and I started laughing so hard we had to put our heads under the covers not to be heard. The man on guard answered offhand that it must have been the tub of excrement that was outside and the wind was blowing the smell into the cabin.

As soon as they left, we wanted to go to our meeting place, but with the threat of the man on guard to inform the Internal Service, we had to wait until he was relieved at 10:00. The guy who replaced him was ready to be freed, one of Cerveille's victims, named Etcheverry. He advised us to wait for the third round that would surely not be long in coming and after that he would wish us luck.

During this short conversation the round arrived. As soon as we were outside we shook Etcheverry's hand and went down to the baths. Imagine our surprise at finding nothing in the meeting place except our packs, minus a missing shirt of mine. They had left without us, ach! And we moped around and left swearing at the guard who had prevented our leaving.

We went back safely to our cabins with our packs. Etcheverry asked us for an explanation just when the fourth round arrived. They noticed nothing. We were not betrayed and I was lucky that my missing shirt, thrown away on the hill, was found in the morning on the seashore by a convict from the last convoy employed as an extra butcher.

In the morning we learned that those whom we thought had left without us had capsized and nearly drowned. They got back to their cabin all wet, to the despair of the slave drivers who could find nothing out about the matter so could punish only two of them with sixty days in the cell because they were betrayed by their wet clothes.

They made this convoy clean the pool near the barracks that occasionally emitted a miasma of fevers, pernicious fits, dysentery, etc. A great many of them died. Those who survived found death a little later in the unhealthy construction sites where they were sent. From this convoy, like the previous, there soon remained no more than a handful.

But the supplier of the penal colony, Society with its iniquities, the cruel mother … isn't it there to fill up the deficit?

# Chapter 4
# To Shake a Friendly Hand

"**A**s for the labor here, it's work or die. And for the food, we are dying of hunger. Here's the menu: two days a week 250 grams of bacalhau, that's a codfish of America, we eat it raw with three centiliters of vinegar and one of oil; two days of stew, canned meat; two days of salted American bacon. Sunday, fresh meat. At dinner, five days a week of soup (warm water) with beans (not cooked), red or white; one day of rice. Seven hundred grams of bread, good in Cayenne and the other penitentiaries, black and inedible in the Islands, and all because they get a lot of flour that is put in the humid storehouses where it perishes. As for the wine, the fourth class has wine two days a week, a quarter liter on Tuesdays and Sundays. The first, second and third classes get a quarter liter every day, unless it is taken away for punishment. For the fifth class there is never any wine and they're used in the hardest labor (how logical). These inequalities by class cause jealousy and conflict in the transportation.

"They steal our stuff. When we arrive, we get a hammock, a blanket for three years, a wool jacket for two years, two cotton jackets for one year, three shirts, three pairs of cotton pants; every six months we should get pants and a shirt; a straw hat for nine months, a pair of shoes for a year. Well! Good, there are those who haven't got anything for two years and you can see men all dressed in rags, barefoot, going around all over town. They just gave out the clothes for us these last few days in the Salvation Islands. I had a right to pants, a shirt, and a hat; they gave me a hat." [From a letter of Duval to his companion in the spring of 1888.]

❊   ❊   ❊

I was put back on chores where they pretty much left me alone. I noticed in the squad that on bacalhau days when they gave us oil and vinegar there were always the same men doing the distribution of provisions and not the ones whose turn it was. There were four strong guys eating together: one was a baker, he brought the bread; another was a gardener, he supplied a few vegetables to make the usual last longer and some lettuce on bacalhau days. That's why they always made a big fuss, stealing a third of the ration of oil and vinegar from the others. Now, one day during the distribution I was one of the last to be served and I pointed out that there was a lot of leftovers and they weren't giving each his due. "They don't deliver it to the storeroom either; on the contrary, they steal as much as they can from us. If you get in on it, we won't get anything at all and we won't be able to eat our bacalhau."

"What, what? You're grumbling and complaining. We measure it out, the spoons are the measure, hold on, here's one extra."

"I am not bought for a spoonful of oil and vinegar, but when you're done I will start the distribution all over again."

"Ha! We'll see about that!"

"It's already seen."

When they finished and put the containers of oil and vinegar on the ground, I took them and started the round, giving to each what was due to him and to them also, telling them, "There's something over and above brute force—there's justice!"

They sat there dumbfounded and did not breathe a word. From that day on they did not make a fuss when it was their turn and no longer tried to monopolize the ration of their comrades, and we became friends. It was the same for the pederasts; I never missed an opportunity to snatch from their hands the poor young men ready to give in for a little bread, tobacco, or whatever. I was happy enough to save a few and make men of them. I experienced a real satisfaction from this.

Every day in the squad we heard nothing but threats of fistfights and knifings. And all this for a piece of bread. "Ach! If I knew who took my bread, I'd rip his guts out," etc. It was not hard to make them understand that since it was the administration that regulated their stomachs, that's who should be listening to them so that there would be no one going hungry, at least for bread; that since the needs of each were not the same—there were some with bigger appetites than others—no bread would be lost or thrown away; that whoever has too much can leave it to those who don't have enough and like that we would have no more conflicts, which the administration encouraged so they could have a good laugh.

This was understood and there were no more fights over the bread.

❖   ❖   ❖

One day the *Cappy* arrived around 4:00 p.m. coming from Cayenne and heading for Maroni. A chore team was put together to unload it and did not return until around 8:00 p.m.

One guy named Derebourg, who had been on board, handed me a letter, a small brochure and the newspaper *Le forçat du travail* [The Slave of Labor]. I was really surprised. I read the letter signed by Victor Cails telling me that in this cursed country there was a comrade who was free, offering me his services in whatever he could do. What joy I felt when Derebourg explained it all to me in his own words! Cails was asking for letters from me to my companion and friends and he would take responsibility for seeing that they were delivered, plus a rough report about the penal colony, the abuses committed therein, etc. I set myself to the task, taking strong precautions and many convicts in my squad backed me up in this.

❊ ❊ ❊

During its first return from Maroni the *Cappy* put in at the Islands to unload some bricks that were going to be used for the construction of new cells. I was lucky to be part of this chore, which was led by a guard and the black transport foreman, a scoundrel of the worst type. For some time rumor had it that the beginning of yellow fever was rampant in Maroni and because of this it was prohibited to go on board and greet whatever crew or passengers there were. Thus I could not meet with comrade Cails. I would have been glad to shake a friendly hand.

Soon after we started unloading, the guard took off with the first barge and we stayed behind under the orders of the Black who demonstrated his authority by yelling at the men at the top of his lungs.

Since I was not paying much attention to my work and constantly staring at the bridge, looking for Cails, for the signal he had given me, in order to exchange at least a sign of collusion with him, he took me aside. At his first words I threatened to smash his head in with some bricks. As he came up to me, I was ready to throw the two I held in my hands at him. He stopped. This scene did not go unnoticed and it attracted the attention of everyone on deck. It was then that I thought I recognized comrade Cails from the greasy mechanic suit, and just in case I asked for him.

"It's me," he said.

"And me, Duval."

"Ah! My poor old man, how are you," etc. "Isn't it too bad that you can't come on board. Ah! The goons, you know very well that it's not true, there's no yellow fever in Maroni. So tell me, what can I get for you?"

"Nothing," I told him. "Besides, we can't accept anything because of this so-called yellow fever."

This kind-hearted man offered the little money he had—I refused. He went to get some tobacco and threw me a few bags. I am thinking, incidentally, that for unloading the bricks during this conversation I had completely stopped working and four or five times had told the Black to go to hell when he tried to keep me from talking. But when Cails tossed me the tobacco, a new altercation broke out and it did not take long to take a turn for the worse. When the Black objected to me taking the tobacco, but could not stop me, Cails and a few passengers (freedmen) laid into him after the threats he made to have them search me on the dock and punish me.

And I answered, "So why did you accept the bag that a passenger from your country (a Bourbonnais) gave you. If I'm forbidden, so are you, and anyway do whatever you want, I couldn't care less. For my part I know what I have to do."

He calmed down. I went back to work all the while continuing to exchange a few words with comrade Cails, whom I would never see again. He advised me to deliver to him as quickly as possible what he had asked of me, which he would deliver on his next voyage.

We returned from the chore and the black foreman did not whisper a word about what happened between us. When I got back to the squad I gave out the tobacco to a few others and not one of us got yellow fever from smoking it.

❋   ❋   ❋

[An excerpt from a letter found in Duval's file in the Archives—it never reached its destination.]

"I know that the reader of this letter, or rather of these notes, is going to be very upset in learning about the way in which we are persecuted here, and me in particular for their hatred of my ideals of equality, liberty, humanity, morality, justice, etc. …

In case they give no satisfaction to your request at the Ministry, which is more than certain—being the wife of an anarchist, they will try to deceive you with honeyed words and especially that word Patience, which they like so much—you'll have to take advantage of the fact that there is now a brave and devoted comrade here to receive your letters; and in his name send four hundred francs. With this if I go to another penitentiary, I can find a little rowboat that will drop me off in a safe place. Even here in the Islands by some other way I'll be able to regain my freedom. And in case you come, send me, while waiting, through this comrade, a payment of fifteen or twenty francs, whatever you can, so I can buy a little tin of tobacco and some food to tide me over. Never send money through the administration, you know they don't give it to me. In the past all the deportees could receive ten francs a month from their families, the penal colony was less bleak, everyone found a way to earn a little money. Today, since the formation of classes—inequalities that they created, even in the Penal Colony—it's utterly miserable. And they plunder and steal everything they can get their hands on.

"It is a sorry environment for a thinker. What do we see: selfishness and denouncement. You, sweet friend, who was so afraid that I was going to the bloody guillotine, if it wasn't for the hope of seeing you again, you can be sure that it is preferable for a thinker to be handed over to the executioner, the legal and official murderer, than to be sent here to the dry guillotine where a good man suffers so cruelly to be separated from his loved ones …

[The letter breaks off, then continues.]

"I want to tell you all that since I've been here in Cayenne, I've seen some newspapers discussing my affair, among others *Le Voltaire* and *Le Figaro*. They were outraged that there were not charges pressed against you, dear comrades, for the respect and sympathy that you showed me in the courtroom on January 12 when you protested against the partiality of Bérard des Glajeux and his consorts … and *Le Temps*, not knowing where to classify me, said that I would probably be classified among the mixed anarchists, saying that the use of the m[ … ] pliers is a specialty that the Anarchist Dictionary has not yet defined (louses and idiots, yes, it's the pliers that will provide the money necessary for you to exterminate them, it's the chief weapon the anarchists should use!). It also said that I and the guy who wanted to blow up the statue of Thiers are the only anarchists who belonged to groups of action and that Gallo was the only one who acted alone, so the real traditions of anarchy belong to him alone. So tell these imbeciles and slimy individuals for me that, although I belonged to a group, I did not ask the permission or approval of any member of the group and that therefore I acted according to my conscience and preserved my individual autonomy.

"Courage, patience and hope."

*　*　*

During this time an escape was being prepared. Eight of us (Lupi, Sevox, Guérin, Austruy, Guidici, Paul, André, and I) were going to leave on the iron barge, which needed a big sail, etc. André was working in the hospital as a nurse, so he was going to provide the sheets to make it.

I did not hide from my escape partners my astonishment that they gave such a responsibility to André, relying on him to be cautious instead of giving him only a limited trust and especially by putting him in danger from the start. They did not agree with me. They trusted him completely. The results taught us who was right.

Everything went according to plan. The sail was made and hidden with a great deal of difficulties, just like the provisions that we needed. The day set for departure was approaching …

The night before, around 6:30, the deportee Paul came up to camp, to my great surprise since he never came up unless he needed something. This time he took me aside and asked me when I was figuring on escaping on the iron barge. I was taken aback by this question. He said that it wasn't good to exclude him because he, too, wanted to leave with me because he knew me, but I obviously did not trust him. I told him it wasn't the case and that if I didn't talk to him about my plans, it was because his situation was not the same, that pretty soon he would be going to Cayenne where he would have a job and that therefore he would have a lot more opportunities than here in the Islands where we desperately tried our luck.

He went along with me and told me that he had not come up to camp to criticize me, but because of what he'd heard from someone who didn't know he'd overheard, which was this: we were betrayed. By whom? A mystery. Slave drivers and soldiers were waiting for us with loaded rifles and would shoot us without warning as soon as we approached the dock.

I beat it out of there and Paul took off. When I got back to the squad I let the inmates in on what I had just learned and right away they decided to get rid of the material proof the next day. Everything was destroyed except the sail, which was impossible to get rid of and, since it was hidden underground closed up in a box, we let it rot. A year later they found it—it had gone to pieces.

They waited for us for a few days, arms at the ready, but to their great despair their victims, whom they had sworn to murder like cowards, did not fall into their trap. They were surprised and disappointed, since they said later that they had all chosen their man and promised not to miss him. The sister in the hospital noticed that some sheets were missing so they searched in every nook and cranny, but found nothing.

During this time Director Vérignon sent letters upon letters to the commandants of the penitentiaries so that they might crack down on the convicts. He prohibited tobacco to the men of the fourth and fifth classes. Whoever was caught smoking or in possession of tobacco would be severely punished.

He gave orders on how they should make their rounds. I do not know if it was the same in the other penitentiaries; I don't think so. But in the Islands the second guards, on their two-hour duty, had to make two rounds. The roll call had to be made in each squad and the men had to get out of their hammocks and answer present. There were ten and sometimes twelve rounds a night, so it was impossible to get any rest. A complaint was made to Commandant Cor, who did not want to hear it.

Nevertheless, it could not go on like this, it was barbaric. The men could not put up with any more. They were falling asleep at their work and the slave drivers were having the time of their lives. They praised the good Director

Vérignon who was providing them with the means to persecute the men. Apart from this a few of them who were less brutish and nasty, wore slippers so that they wouldn't make too much noise in the cabins.

It had been decided among some of the squad that if this continued, they would refuse to get out of their hammocks and answer "present."

A few days after this decision, on a Sunday when I was glum, I had not talked to anyone and was leaning against the side of the water tank watching the magnificent sunset (which is very frequent in this place and most of the time took my mind off things). My mind was wandering far from that hell when the twilight fell a little before I went back at 7:00 p.m. I returned quiet and thoughtful to the squad. I passed by the guard named Chaoutier, who said nothing to me. When I was close to the squad, he called out me and told me to follow him to the prison.

"Why?" I asked. "I'm not late, bedtime hasn't sounded, and it's not for being noisy because I haven't talked to anyone since roll call."

"It's not for that."

"For what then?"

"I don't know anything about it. Anyway, it's no big deal, you'll get out tomorrow."

The prison foreman (an Arab who spoke French very well. Moreover, he had been a sergeant and was only known by this name) searched me and found four or five cigarettes' worth of tobacco.

Chaoutier said to me, "You see, Duval, if I made a report you would be punished for this tobacco, but I think that's stupid since we ourselves give some to the convicts when they do chores for us like carrying baggage and stuff."

They put me in the cell, with irons on my feet only, and when I was well chained Chaoutier said to me, "You don't know, Duval, eh, this cell has been waiting for you since this morning."

In fact, I found out later that around 8:00 a.m. they had taken out the guy named Sevox, who was serving a fifteen-day punishment for stealing vegetables (being a gardener, he had taken a few radishes). The next morning

I got out and around 1:00 p.m. the slave driver Chaoutier told me I got thirty days for stealing tobacco. The boss guard Moretti, who did not want to see me in the camp, fearing an escape, had given the order to stick me in the cell during the day at the slightest infraction of regulations. Since I did not commit any, he took advantage of those few cigarettes to make a report.

They continued to wake the men up at every round. One time Austruy and Paul refused to get up and answer the roll. Right away they were thrown in the cell.

We had a visit from the Director Vérignon, decorated with his medals and with his sword at his side. I was in cell number 2 and in number 1 was a guy called Novarez, who had been sentenced to death for stabbing another convict. It was later commuted to five years in double chains. Commandant Cor, who accompanied the Director, stopped at every cell and named the prisoner and the reason for his punishment. Close to mine, even though they were almost whispering, I heard Commandant Cor say, "That's Duval, the anarchist, a very dangerous man. He's doing thirty days for stealing tobacco."

Vérignon came to the door, right in front of me, and said, "There are no anarchists here, there are only convicts. If Duval behaves himself, he will earn the benevolence of the administration. But if he doesn't, he and all the Duvals like him will bend to my will."

I answered him that mindful men, such as I considered myself, were like glass—they might break, but they never bend. He said nothing, continued his round and when he passed by my cell again he threw me a hateful glance.

Austruy and Paul were in custody waiting for the Council. They had managed to unchain themselves, break through the roof of their cells and try to escape. Not having the time to prepare their raft as they needed, they nearly drowned and were put back in the cell. Both of them were nice to Commandant Cor, especially Austruy, whom he advised to behave himself well, etc. Austruy answered as he should have.

One day Cor came to pay me a visit along with an officer of the administration and he said to me, "So, Duval, you were wrong this time; you thought you were dealing with friends on board the *Cappy*, but they betrayed you.

Everything you delivered to them has ended up in the hands of the administration and the Governor. Your writings are going to be sent to the Ministry. Ha! Buddy, you are nowhere close to leaving here, it's ninety days in the hole waiting for you. In the Ministry they don't take these things lightly."

I told him that I would gladly sign up for six months in the cell if I were sure that those few truths got out. But, ha! I didn't have to worry about them sending it to the Ministry. "They don't show off a jacket that's not good."

The officer of the administration smiled at me in approval. Cor made them close my cell without breathing a word. When they had left I wondered what all this meant. Certainly my writings had been seized. But how? Was comrade Cails careless? Were we betrayed by some convicts? I longed to find out about the matter when I got out of the cell. Here's what I learned.

While traveling through the Islands to Cayenne, the captain of the *Cappy* had forced open Cails's trunk while he was in the stokehold, taken the writings, read them and sent them to the Governor. When Cails noticed this he became furious and wanted to throw the captain overboard. He still went to Maroni, but on the return trip they made him take the mail boat back to France. As for me, they would not talk to me about it anymore and I never learned how the captain of the *Cappy* had found out about the delivery of these papers to comrade Cails.

Commandant Cor was called back to Cayenne where he resumed his duty as head clerk. Paul and Austruy took the same boat to be court-martialed for their escape attempt. It was during this crossing that they learned from Commandant Cor that it was André who had betrayed us in the escape with the barge.

Austruy was surprised and said, "It's not possible since he was supposed to have gone down with us—then he would have been shot, too?"

"No, no, my naïve little fool! In fact, how come you didn't go down? Ah, they were waiting for you ..."

"In a trap," Austruy said.

"We have to guard you, not let you escape."

"Yes, but not murder us like cowards. Your duty was to watch us, to prevent us from doing it, that's all. Don't you have the cells and irons? That's enough."

"We didn't put you all in cells because we didn't find material evidence."

"No, it's only because of André, because you would have had to put him in also."

"Exactly. So, now that you have nothing to fear in this matter anymore, tell me, where is the sail hidden?"

"Ha, Commandant, now that's a joke!"

Such is the dialogue that Austruy and Paul reported to me and they were sentenced to two to three years in double chains and sent back to the Salvation Islands.

# Chapter 5
# The Guillotine's Blade

After the escape of the boatmen the construction manager told me that Blanc, who was sentenced to hard labor for life and about to finish his five-year stint in double chains, had made a request to the management to be sent to the workshop in Maroni where the work was more important.

"It's going to be granted to him. He'll leave in a little while. Since we've got no worker of his profession to replace him here, I thought of you and I hope that you won't turn it down."

"For you, Mister Dufaure, I wouldn't, but for the administration of the penitentiary, yes. Because I will never take any part in doing the work that Blanc did: bars of justice, shackles, putting double or single chains on convicts for punishment, sharpening the guillotine's blade, etc. I thank you for the interest you show me in offering this work that I would certainly be better at than at the chores that everyone does, but my refusal [to do certain jobs] would carry with it serious punishments for me that I am not at all ready to accept."

"You're wrong, Duval, you're wrong."

"In your opinion, but not in mine."

"Okay, but since I need a convict I can trust, I thought of you for another chore that I think you won't mind too much. This year there's a big drought, so there's no more water in the pool and the drinking water in the tank is wasted by the boys of the guards' families who wash their clothes with it. The Commandant is afraid there may be a water shortage and has put me in charge of going every day to get some barrels of water on Saint Joseph Island and told me to take you with me, if I don't need you anywhere else. How would you like that?"

"Certainly, Mr. Dufaure, you'll need two other responsible men with you."

"Do you know two convicts capable of helping you?"

"Yes."

"Well then, all three of you be at the dock tomorrow morning. When the transport guard brings the provisions to Saint Joseph, I'll give the order to the Interior Service that they should let you go down; that way you won't have any trouble. I will be in the dinghy of provisions that will tow a barge containing four barrels and you three, as well as a pump."

That was the best time I had during my entire captivity. One day we installed the pump in a well, the next day in another. We filled up our four barrels, rolled them to the dock and then at four o'clock the dinghy came to tow the barge and the men from Royal Island rolling the barrels to the camp where they distributed the water.

I don't remember how long I was at this chore, around six weeks, I think. Then, when Blanc had gone to Maroni, Mr. Dufaure called me to his place, offered me a glass of wine, congratulated me on the work, as well as the two men whom I had taken with me, and gave me six packs of tobacco for the three of us.

"Now, mule head," he said to me, "you won't refuse to go to the workshop anymore. The Commandant feels okay toward you, and me too, so you can be sure to have no troubles and you'll go up a class. It's agreed, isn't it, and I'll go inform the Commandant to classify you in the construction work."

"I beg you, Mr. Dufaure, don't do anything. You'll force me to refuse and I'll be punished and like that I'll turn your good intentions toward me into harm."

"Okay, I'll do nothing, mule."

At this time, after the roll call at 5:00 p.m., the convicts could walk around the camp until 7:00 in the evening. Almost every evening I went to the water tank plateau to admire the beautiful sunsets that are around there. Around six weeks after this talk with the construction manager, an Arab foreman came looking for me in the cabin. Not finding me there he came to the water tank and told me that the Commandant had sent him to find me. I saw him in the camp near the construction along with the staff officer of the Islands, the construction manager, the head guard, the administration officer, the chaplain, and the works guard.

The Commandant told me, "Duval, the *Cappy* has to come here the day after tomorrow to transport Blanc, who is employed in the works, to take him to Maroni. Being the only one here of his profession to replace him, you'll go to the works tomorrow morning after the march so that he can give you the equipment inventory that you'll be responsible for."

"Commandant, I'm surprised at your decision because I've had the opportunity to tell you the reasons why I don't want to practice my profession, and since the opportunity presents itself again I will repeat that I will never do any work that might worsen the pain of my comrades in Gehenna, and therefore I'll be punished and maybe worse. I thank you, but under these conditions I absolutely refuse to go to the works."

And I named a convict, an ass well worthy to replace Blanc.

"As long as I am in charge of the penitentiary, he will never go to the works and will have no employment."

"But he's a good servant. The guards use him to haggle with his comrades in misfortune and for false reports from his denunciation which you follow up on."

"Okay, be quiet and don't be stubborn like a mule. The free personnel here don't mean you any harm. I promise that you will go up a class every six months and that you will only have to wait two years to be granted concessions and you'll see your companion whom you love so much. Let's go, Duval, don't be stubborn, all's not lost. Don't try to escape anymore and I'll keep my word. Before these gentlemen I agree to it, as well as to exempt you from doing any work that has anything to do with discipline. You don't have to worry about being forced to put shackles on your comrades' feet, sharpening the guillotine's blade, or anything like that. Let's go, Duval, it's agreed, tomorrow morning you will go to the works."

"Commandant, under such conditions I cannot refuse and if you do what you promise, I'll try not to escape during the period of time I need to be granted concessions. Two years, you say. My word is a sure guarantor for yours."

He dismissed me and the next day the deportee Blanc, in the presence of the works manager, gave me the inventory of equipment that I would be responsible for in the future.

In the beginning I had to struggle hard to put up with the slave drivers, but the Commandant kept his word, taking no heed of their harassment. Knowing full well what was happening because I was watched very closely by some of his faithful servants, I gave them no opportunity to catch me ...

❖   ❖   ❖

The works guard was replaced by a new arrival named Genail, a carpenter. We saw right away that he was a workingman and did not feel comfortable in this environment.

One day he summoned me into his office to give me a work order and he called me "Sir." I mentioned to him that the word did not shock me, that on the contrary it spoke in his favor, but in the future he should watch out using this word with a convict in front of his colleagues or he would be made a laughingstock; likewise before a convict who may repeat it to his comrades who will do the same.

"You're very lucky that it's only the two of us and that the works accountant is not in the office. Otherwise, you would quickly see the proof of what I'm telling you."

He thanked me and we discussed the work, the transportation, and such like things.

The deportees Lupi, Guidici, and Guérin of my squad asked me if I wanted to be part of an escape that they were going to try.

"Yes, if it's under the right conditions. As before if it's agreed to take a dinghy, maybe this time the men won't be so cowardly. If it's a raft, I'm not so sure. I don't trust it. What's more, after the promises of the Commandant, I'm going to see how he will act and take my time to leave here under safer conditions."

"You're right," they told me, "because it is in fact a raft that we want to take, in desperation. You know, there aren't a lot of chances. Here's our plan. On the dock there are some big, long fir beams. We can take four of them if you're with us. Three will be enough. But we have to make them hold together solidly. We were counting on you for this, but now after saying no, are you afraid of risking it?"

"Not at all. I'll go down to the dock to measure the width of the beams and I'll cut four bars of flat iron in which I'll pierce holes for screws that I'll give you and I'll keep it all ready for you."

All three shook my hand. Ah! Such handshakes given wholeheartedly in such a case is well worth risking sixty days in the cell.

Eight days after this discussion, they came to shake my hand again before leaving. They managed to get to sea: an hour later they were after them. The black night worked in their favor and during the day the lost were cast ashore.

After great difficulties landing because they had been seen, they were arrested right away and the dinghy that was chasing them brought them to the Islands in a sorry state. And what ill treatments these unfortunate men suffered, what humiliations!

The raft was brought in tow.

In the interrogation, they didn't fail to ask them who had supplied the iron bands. Not wanting to implicate me, since they were men of honor, they said that they had had these bands of iron made a long time ago—by whom? They wouldn't say.

Since this was denying the evidence, the Commandant was not fooled. The proof was that after his departure for Cayenne to appear before the Council—which cost Lupi and Guérin two years each in double chains, both being sentenced to life; Guidici, with a limited sentence, was extended two years—the Commandant sent for me.

"Duval," he said, "I'm happy with you. You kept your word by not leaving with your friends."

"But, Commandant …"

"Hush, I know everything."

And he reported to me almost word for word the discussion before their departure.

"Are you also going to deny that it was you who supplied them with what they needed? The evidence is there, except for the screwdriver that you made for them, which we haven't found yet. Hey, you see how well informed I am! Nevertheless, I won't crack down on you since I understand your situation and you didn't leave this time with those whom you had already tried to escape with a few times before. I know you can't do otherwise. But being the Commandant of the penitentiary, I ought to punish you severely."

"Commandant, I don't have the same reasons as my comrades in misfortune to deny my involvement in their escape attempt, seeing that they did not want to implicate me, on the contrary I will admit it and I would have been glad if they had succeeded. I'm sorry that they failed and for the added suffering that it causes them, but I'm not sorry at all for the days or months of solitary that you might want to inflict on me."

"I'll tell you again that this time you won't be punished. But, what I don't understand is that you put yourself in this position to be punished for the likes of these men, stranglers like Lupi and Guérin, and that Guidici who is not much better."

"Ah! Commandant, you're like all men with their social situations or their positions, and the ensuing authoritative principles—you believe you have authority over other men and you catalogue them as this or that, only looking at the effects and not the causes. As for me, Commandant, I deny free will. A combination of circumstances has made these men what they are. In other circumstances they may have been different and not have acted in the same way. What I have observed with respect to these men whom you have described like this is that at a particular moment they were rogues, I don't defend this. But at other times they act like honorable men. Their conduct in the penitentiary and what they have just done with respect to me prove it. Therefore, these men—and so many others, *unfortunately*—in some other environment or surroundings may have been types of elite. Their energy and their strength of character prove this. All the unfortunate men who are here are atoning for the faults of the defective society in which we live. That cruel mother, in the struggle for life, annihilates the higher sentiments in individuals to make room for evil instincts. That's how they drill their way through life and some get the title of 'honest man' while others get called 'convict,' like your servant, Commandant."

"It's your own fault."

"Yes, because I was clumsy and couldn't manage to do what I wanted to do. Too bad …"

I went back to work. Two months later the escapees returned from Cayenne and they were happy that things went the way they did for me. They were put back in the third squad—incorrigibles and fifth class—where I was. They told me what happened during the escape and advised me, especially because of my rheumatism, never to try to leave under such conditions.

I took advantage of the opportunity to make them understand and feel how wrong they had been to let the sails and provisions perish, the ones I kept hidden when I was working on the dock and that they were hurting for boldness and energy: it was so easy to get hold of a dinghy.

I told them, "And today we would probably be free, instead of vegetating, wilting away, slumping in this foul cesspool from which neither you nor

I will ever leave except by paying nature its indispensable tribute. Excuse my criticism because it certainly isn't courage that you lack, you just proved that. But at that time you were scared of bullets, which, however, were less to be feared than these things, given the distance that we could have put between the sharpshooters and us. It's this fear and the lack of boldness that made us miss such a good chance that we will never have again."

"It's true," they told me, "we have to admit it. But all is not lost. We can start again and this time after such a lesson there will be no hesitation."

"I'm afraid that right now I have no confidence. For my part I'm going to do what I told you when you escaped."

"You're right. With a little patience you'll get off the Islands and be granted concessions and then ..."

"For that the Commandant has to keep his word for me to go up a class every six months. The appointment will take place soon and we'll see. If nothing happens, I don't care, I'll leave right away all alone on a plank of wood rather than wait for schemes that always abort at the last minute."

This moment of disgust, doubt, lassitude, and failure proved to me the resilient character and kindness of my comrades in misfortune who, seeing me in such a state, did their best to chase it away. They shook my hand and said, "Oh, no! We respect you too much to let you leave under such conditions. If things don't go the way you want, we'll all leave together."

And these were the pariahs, the rejects of society who spoke such words! And all the time we've heard, "He's a bad man, he was born bad ..."

❖ ❖ ❖

July 14, 1889. The authorities of the penitentiary attended the roll call for the appointment of classes.

They began with declassing the incorrigibles, I was one of them and I was satisfied. The Commandant had kept his word. But I was thinking of the road I would have to travel to go from fifth to first class: accepting that I could pass regularly every six months, it was still two years of waiting. That seemed so long to me! I couldn't believe it, then, when I heard my name called again to pass from fifth to fourth class. That was six months gone that I wasn't counting on. Just then I caught sight of the Commandant who looked very satisfied and seemed to say, "I have kept my word and even more."

After roll call the order was given to change my squad. Ha! What congratulations from my comrades in Gehenna, how happy they were. "Patience, courage, you'll get out of here, you'll see your companion whom you love so much," etc. They were the ones who picked up my hammock and packed my bag. Then, when everything was ready, some of them grabbed me and put me on the shoulders of a butcher whose name I don't remember, just his nickname: The Hunter, because he had done his service as a hunter in Africa.

Then the entire squad went with me. We crossed the camp to go to the squad across from the military hospital, the first or second squad. (Writing these lines of an almost twenty-year-old memory, I am still moved when thinking about these poor, good-natured men almost all dead in that hell after so much suffering.)

The guard on duty wanted to block our passage and make the men go back to their cabin. He had to be satisfied with making a report. The men paid no attention to him despite his threats and they yelled, "You won't stop us from taking Duval into his new squad! He's not an ass, that's not why he went up a class, it's for his work, because it was his right, etc. He's not like so-and-so or so-and-so, ha! The pigs, like the watchdogs, earn their stripes by making false reports, by murdering us." And so on.

We finally got to the squad and I was quickly set up. Then it was agreed that when I got the first quarter liter of wine, everyone from the old squad would come and have a taste. It didn't happen like that, but it was split in three and downed.

The guard was outraged that we hadn't obeyed his stupid threats, so he made a ludicrous report that turned the whole Internal Service and all the slave drivers upside down when all they wanted to do was have fun on the national holiday. Also, there was a racket in the camp. The Commandant had to intervene, so he summoned me and asked what had happened.

"That's it," he said. "I'm not surprised, I was expecting that."

He tore up the report and everything went back to order.

And he told me, "I hope, Duval, that you're going to participate in the celebration, in the games that I've let them organize at the request of several convicts. It'll be fun and I'll be there to enjoy myself too."

"Excuse me, Commandant, maybe it's your place, but not mine. It's your role, not mine."

"Come on, Duval, you should be happy and not be so stubborn."

I returned to the squad, which was soon deserted by everyone except two guys who kept me company. Then boredom got the best of us and we wanted to get away from the crazy laughter of the executioners' victims, so we went to take a walk on the covered path. Two slave drivers and two foremen blocked our way and we had to turn around and go back to camp.

Automatically stopped by one guy or another, we watched the celebration, which was not too bad considering what little means the organizers had at their disposal and their initiative hampered by the slave drivers. There was a little bit of everything, like a little country fair.

On the orders of the Commandant, they left the men free to have their fun until 10:00 p.m.; they simply watched out for escapes. Everyone on both sides was satisfied, but it was the first and the last celebration I saw in the Salvation Islands. Vérignon, the new director, thinking only of irons, cells, holes, and the guillotine, did not want this to happen again and even for this one time berated Commandant Leloup. For the rest of the year 1889 there was nothing out of the ordinary concerning me. I was relatively peaceful.

There were constant arrivals of unfortunate men from the construction works around Cayenne, Kourou, Pariacabo, etc., all in a pitiable state. The few who pulled through told us about the way they were mistreated in those death camps.

Hearing these tales in which we sensed so much cowardice on the part of these men who had given up, we wondered whether the victims were really any better than the executioners. For myself, I did not hide the contempt I felt for certain things suffered by them without revolting, before being completely sapped and beaten down by fevers. All this was repeated to the Commandant who reproached me. But still, I did not hide my outrage at the villainy on the one side or the cowardice on the other.

"So don't worry about it, it'll just cause you trouble."

"Ah! Commandant, so it's everywhere and in every situation that they tout personal interest in order to smother the spirit of justice among individuals."

&ast; &ast; &ast;

In January 1890 the appointment of classes took place and I went up to third class, which gave me the right to a quarter liter of wine and two sous every day. The construction manager and the Commandant, in order to increase my pay, gave me an apprentice for whom I got six sous a day. I put a third of this pay in a nest egg and I pocketed the other two. Thus I had six or seven francs coming to me at the end of the month. [ ... ]

I spoke above about some disagreements between Governor Gerville-Réache and Director Vérignon, as well as the antipathy and contempt of some individuals and of all the bigwigs of the Colony.

Vérignon had no friends except in the administrative personnel. And who? Those in whom he could inspire fear, knowing that he had a good reputation in the Ministry for his bluff as a splendid reformer in the penitentiary service. Everything he proposed to his hierarchical bosses was everything that could possibly be inhuman, barbaric, and cruel toward the unfortunate victims of our social condition and especially in such a country and in such a climate. Everything was accepted by these "Gentlemen" and Vérignon the Hyena was sent back to Guiana with full powers—to the utter astonishment of those who had not lost all feeling of humanity and dignity. For a coward, a traitor, whatever he may be and wherever on the top or the bottom of the social ladder, is always a coward and a traitor. This was the opinion of the VIPs of Cayenne who protested in every way when they learned of his return and of the departure of Governor

Gerville-Réache who was well respected and whose recall by the Ministry was not understood.

So, what crime had he committed? That of not having the ferocity of a brute like the boss of the "Pen." He proved this during his trip across the colony to the different penitentiaries and construction sites. He came to the Salvation Islands accompanied by Commandant Campana, the acting director in the interim. What complaints were made to him! He did his best to give satisfaction to those that seemed better founded to him, but really, if he had done the same for every one, not a single convict would have remained in the Islands.

He was not insensitive to the double chained [where the convict chained by the feet was chained to the hammock at night], who were all sent to the Islands at Vérignon's wish. He promised to send them to new construction sites that had to be opened for a railroad track going from Maroni to Cayenne, an excavation work where most were bound to die. Oh well. There was hope on the mainland, whereas on the Islands—nothing to do.

While waiting to leave, for those who did not have any punishment for some time and for those who had three months before having any, orders were given to take off the chains of the first, leaving them simply in shackles, and the same for the second for the three months to spend without punishment.

On his return, Vérignon was scandalized at this kindness toward such dangerous convicts. He made a ludicrous report about it against the Governor, who was recalled by the Ministry right away. The day after his departure a circular was sent to all the heads of the penitentiaries and construction works that they had to immediately put the chains back on the men who had benefited from this measure that was taken with no regard for common sense or the proper functioning of the Law, the regulations, discipline, etc.

Before the governor came by my squad, we had a visit from Commandant Campana who talked with me for the first time. With all the promises he made I concluded that he was a bootlicker and I only said to him that I asked for nothing but my rights. Since I was subjected to the strictness of the regulations like everyone else I should have the same benefits. "The administration only has to honor its commitment, I will honor mine."

"Yes, but you know …" This conversation was cut short by the arrival of a guard who came to inform Campana that the Governor was arriving in the camp.

In the squad of classed men, there were also quite a few complaints. I was, maybe, the only one who did not complain about anything. The Director and Commandant Leloup made the Governor stop in front of my hammock and told him my name.

"Ah! This is the anarchist Duval who thought he could get away with writing clandestine letters, if you can call those letters—it'd be better to say books. You know, I found out about your prolific correspondence seized on board the *Cappy* and many others besides. It's a very serious case in your situation and I could have punished you severely for it. I did not do so, but in the future don't try to write like that, secretly, because everything will be handed over to me and the next time without any consideration I will act without pity."

"Governor, I've never asked for anything and will never ask anyone for consideration or pity. I was guided by the spirit of justice because I was outraged at seeing the abuses and injustices that are committed here and that I believed had to be brought to light. I made the most of writing the eighty-two pages and other letters of ten or twelve pages. It was only the cowardice and betrayal of someone that made them fall into your hands. You didn't clamp down, you say, because your conscience opposed it. But you're not unaware, at least in general, of what goes on in this hell. And in the question of details you should know enough after all the different complaints that every convict made to you when you passed by them. As for me, I have no complaint to make. For the time being they leave me alone, they don't intercept my letters and I receive my correspondence on a regular basis, restricted to one letter a month addressed to my companion. From friends I have never received any, the regulations forbid it."

After my speech the Governor turned to Commandant Leloup and asked him if I was behaving well. When the Commandant said yes, he turned around right away and said, "That's good, we will grant him concessions, isn't that right, gentlemen?"

But when walking away he added, "He still has some seeds in his head."

As a response I yelled out that I would preserve these seeds forever, as they were given to me by men of noble and generous sentiments, fighting for an ideal as wonderful as anarchy.

The interim director Campana came back to me, took me by the arm and said, "Be quiet, be quiet, fool, don't answer like that. They're feeling good about you, you'll screw it up."

"I don't care, my answer isn't insolent or arrogant. It's a desire that these seeds that Mr. Governor talks about be in the heads of all individuals, then we would see a little more equality and happiness—there's enough for everyone on earth …"

"Okay, Duval, I'll come back through the Islands and see you later."

On Vérignon's arrival, he resumed his duty as High Commandant in Maroni and continued to protect the Chinese. Later he returned to France or was sent to another colony. I never saw him again.

# Chapter 6
# A Most Unusual Stash

The last two convoys brought some comrades: [Léon] Lepiez, [Joseph] Paridaën, [Charles-Antoine, called Biscuit or Ravachol II] Simon, Chevenet, Faugoux, and Thiervoz. The last was a sympathizer to whom the comrades had propagandized during the crossing, especially Simon, whom he highly respected, seeing him being so young, sincere, and convincing. The construction work for the Incarceration on Saint Joseph Island had begun, so the new arrivals disembarked on this island. To my great regret, this prevented me from seeing them and getting news from France or some propaganda, which I was eager for.

✻ ✻ ✻

The first comrade whose hand I shook was our unfortunate comrade [Anthelme] Girier-Lorion whose arrest is described on page 200 of the book *Souvenirs du Bagne* by Liard-Courtois [1903], as Girier himself told me. No use going back over the matter. But, let it be said in passing, there will never be enough disgust, contempt, and hatred against Delori and all those who had a hand in the arrest of our lamented friend, treated as a snitch by the cowards and ambitious idiots. For the anarchist idea it was the loss of an apostle, by virtue of his eloquence and the firmness and sincerity of his convictions.

❁　❁　❁

He had sent word to me through a convict coming to the Islands to tell me that he was in Maroni. The deportee Navals was being sent to this penitentiary, so I gave him a long letter with the information that he asked of me.

A little later, I was surprised when a convict working at the water tank to turn the wheel of a Pasteur [or Chamberland] filter came to tell me that a man coming from Maroni was asking after me.

"Who is it?"

"I don't know. What I do know is that he's assigned to the stone cabin. He's waiting at the water tank for the guard and the foreman to open the door for him."

Since Gosset was there, I told him to go get this fellow or else I would go find him.

"Considering the guard on duty, it's better if you go," Gosset told me.

I went there right away and found myself face to face with Girier who, also being happy to shake a friendly hand, threw himself in my arms and we hugged. (As I write these lines and recall the memory and the suffering of this good, sincere comrade, I have tears in my eyes.)

In the stone cabin he took a place near mine and we had endless conversations and discussions. I was truly surprised at his eloquence, and him so young. He talked for a long time about our good comrade Pierre Martin whom he highly respected. He had known him in Vienna and he told me about the trial with comrades Tennevin and Buisson. Together we figured out a way to communicate with the comrades on Saint Joseph Island. Oh! Selfishness, I was almost happy not to be feeling alone on this rock anymore …

Girier, who until then had been in good health apart from a few bouts of fever, fell sick and had such a high fever that they had to rush him to the infirmary. This was due to the sunburn that he got on the boat when they put him in irons. Since they did not want to give him anything to relieve himself, he held it in for more than forty-eight hours, which caused troubles in his organs, resulting in persistent constipation and diarrhea.

He left the infirmary after three weeks, sicker than when he had entered. He continued to have intermittent fevers every three days and was unable to do any hard labor. In order to have him, like me, well guarded they put him at the Pasteur filter. I got some medicine and condensed milk from an employee at the pharmacy and made him bread soup on the cattleman's stove. We also got a little salad. All this helped him recuperate a little and he cheered up a bit. I helped him a lot with that, pretending to be in a good mood and giving him hope of better days when we could, maybe, be useful to the ideas that were so dear to us. This brought him back to life. He smiled and shook my hand effusively. I felt that I really had a good friend there and that I reciprocated because I loved Girier like my own son. Ah! How happy and proud I would be if I had one like him.

In the same convoy as the comrades the deportee [Charles] Todd, an Englishman, also disembarked on Royal Island. He was put in the stone cabin and was immediately recognized by [Henry] Sevox, with whom he was in Saint Martin de Ré [an island in western France] in 1884 or 1885: Todd was waiting to leave for New Caledonia where he had to serve a twenty-year sentence of hard labor [for housebreaking and burglary] and Sevox was waiting to go to Guiana, sentenced to life for murder.

❊　❊　❊

In the way they shook each other's hand we felt that there was a mutual trust and respect between them, which did not take long to show itself. Todd seemed bothered and overexcited. I knew the reason before too long.

Todd had money and knew that the administration was suspicious, so he feared that they would put him in solitary and make him swallow a purgative. He asked Sevox to keep his stash for him. He refused because he was also suspect and so susceptible to being searched at any minute. "But I know someone who will help out."

Sevox, having set his sight's on me, found me and asked me if I wanted to help Todd out, "who, as you can appreciate, deserves it. He's a very good man." I accepted and an hour later I was holding a silver stash (what Liard-Courtois calls the convict's safe). I had already seen some made of zinc by a tinsmith, but this was the first time I had one in my hands, a pretty one, very clean and with unusual contents: there were three hundred francs in gold, some twenty-franc coins, four thousand-franc bills, four hundred-franc bills, and a ring worth fifteen hundred francs. Being responsible for such a sum for a comrade in misfortune worried me and I didn't sleep that night. To keep it together the next day at the march, I had a feeling that is still as vivid today.

The Captain of Arms made me wait and led me to the Internal Service. Immediately my thought was that some rat had seen me take the stash and had informed the guard on the night round without me noticing and that they were taking me to the Internal Service to search me. It was impossible to get rid of the money. Ah! What convulsions ran through me in that minute-long walk!

And what relief I felt when the guard Raymond told me to set aside the machetes that were damaged beyond repair, as well as the hoes, shovels, and axes and to make a list of what I needed as far as handles, to bring it to him and the next day he would get some men on chores to take these old tools to the store until the Commission came by (which noted down what was worn-out and had it thrown into the sea. I saw brand new tools thrown away that they didn't want to give out and that they let rot in the store. Ah! Good taxpayers, what a waste, and all this happened at the convicts' expense).

After distributing the tools to the men on chores accompanied by their guards, I temporarily hid the money I was entrusted with and during the siesta I had a talk with Todd, who told me not to leave the ring in the stash, but to hide it separately, as well as the gold and two one-hundred-franc bills because, he said, "I may need a certain sum at one time or another and also to buy what we'll need to improve our sorry fare."

"Todd, speak for yourself and not in the plural. I'm helping you out because I believe you deserve it and not out of self-interest. My fare is enough for me."

"Come on, Duval, you won't refuse me the pleasure of breaking bread together sometimes—with me, Sevox, and two or three others—with what we can get."

His invitation was made in good faith and with all sincerity, which Girier and I accepted a few times. He had great respect for little Simon and every time I bought tobacco for him, fifty packs at a time, he told me to send some to Saint Joseph for Simon and his comrades to smoke.

This convict was truly a good man, with a big heart. Everything he had he shared with whomever he respected. He was educated, handsome, part of a band of gentlemen thieves, wearing gloves and blowing up the safes of banks and wealthy bourgeoisie. They took from those who had and not from whose who had not, like so many miserable wretches do, I should say, attacking the poor devil who struggles for a week or a month and whom they knock down to take the modest sum earned with so much difficulty and that his wife and kids are waiting for impatiently.

In 1869 my father, after ten days of work and staying up sometimes until midnight or 2:00 a.m. to meet his deadlines and leave nothing undone, got ninety-two francs for his work. At 9:00 p.m. one night he was assaulted by four individuals armed with clubs and they knocked him out, took his clothes, left him with nothing but his shirt, and buried him in a pile of manure. (That saved his life—the manure stuck to the wounds and stopped the bleeding.) At 3:00 in the morning he was found by a milkman who saw spots of blood on the road, stopped his horse and found my father. A colleague helped him put my father in the car and he brought him to his house and right away went to get a doctor who thought my father was a goner. Three days later, however, he recovered consciousness and was brought home.

During those three days my mother was inconsolable and I thought I was going to lose her. For my part, I ran around day and night going to the worst dive bars in order to get some word, some hint that would set me on the trail of my father's murderers because I was convinced that he had been the victim of a night attack. For a long time I tried to shed some light on the suspicions I had about certain individuals of the district, but I could never find anything out and my father could not recognize any of his assailants. Without that, he had no more recourse to the law than I did, so there was never any complaint filed. But I would have served justice myself by killing the rogues. Yes, rogues! But why so? To whom, to what should we attribute the responsibility, if not to our social state that has always been so defective, so hard on the disinherited, the bruised, the crushed who cannot or do not know how to react against their surroundings, thus handing down to us their flaws through atavism and heredity …

❖   ❖   ❖

Todd and his gang were men who had received a good education and up-bringing, but distorted, finding that everything was for the best in the best of worlds. Girier and I had some discussions with him that we had to drop in order not to anger him because he was ignorant of sociology. He was bourgeois, looking for a good time, but with an upright, loyal nature. After eating up his inheritance he wanted to keep leading a life in the fast lane and so he joined up with this gang. They did good business.

One day Todd was arrested, (I don't know the circumstances), and was sentenced to twenty years of hard labor for aggravated robbery. His friends helped him escape from New Caledonia and a few years later he was caught again in France while unloading a safe. Of course he had changed his name and was not recognized, was sentenced again to twenty years of hard labor and this time was sent to Guiana. He did not go before the Council for escaping because nobody knew him except for Sevox, Lupi, Girier, and me. No slips were made by any of us. He was calm and feared only one thing: that a guard from New Caledonia would come to Guiana and recognize him. Four years after the fact he recognized two, but they didn't recognize him.

Thinking that the money was not safe in the tool crib, I armed myself one morning with a hammer, scissors, and some prepared cement, and went to the stone cabin knowing that the watch was alone. I sent him to the hospital to get us some coffee. I had calculated that it would take ten minutes, or more if there was a snag with a guard or some kind of ass. For once that would be useful for something by giving me time to make a hole under my hammock to hide the stash with the four one-thousand-franc bills and the ring in another hole under Girier's hammock in the corner. I finished sealing up both holes before the cabin watch returned. In case I had an accident I had told Girier about it and shown him the hiding places.

He said to me, "If no one else knows about this, if no one saw you, then they'd have to be pretty crafty if they wanted to get this money because you can't see a thing."

I had gone through all that trouble and taken precautions for nothing. A little later Todd told me to fix it so I wouldn't have any problems getting the money because he might need it at any time. So another morning I used the same strategy and took out the stash to hide it again back in the tool crib where I made a hole twenty inches deep. The ring was easier to get and I left it above Girier's hammock.

Then Todd asked me, "Do you think that with the help of the boatmen it would be easy to leave in the middle of the day with the dinghy?"

"Certainly. It's even possible without the help of the boatmen. If you're bold enough and strong enough you have a chance to succeed, but with the help of the boatmen you're sure to leave the Islands and gain your freedom, if you meet no accidents on the way."

"Okay, my friend, that's how we're going to get out of here, Sevox, Lupi, and Girier, if, that is, they're willing to go out of their way for us, you, me, and three boatmen, one of whom the guard Le Goff trusts, a Breton like him and a very good sailor whom I promised five hundred francs if we succeed.

He and the other two are thrilled to leave with all of us. We're going to start making the sail right away and I hope we'll be leaving soon."

Sevox told Lupi, who was in the hospital, and I told Girier, who accepted, but happier for me than for himself, saying that he was young and he could do his time whereas mine had no end.

The business did not go as quickly as we had hoped, no doubt due to something leaking out. The three boatmen noticed that they were watched more closely than usual. Therefore, it was impossible to make the sail and for us in the camp it was the same. The surveillance finally let up and the sail was made and hidden until the right moment for the escape because it was necessary to fix things up so we could put as much luck as possible on our side—not to be met by boats that could capture us.

But while waiting, a setback happened that ruined us. A flu epidemic struck first on Royal Island and then on Saint Joseph and Devil's Island. On the latter two it was mild, but on Royal Island more than half of the men were affected, many fatally. The epidemic threw everything into confusion; it would have been a help rather than a hindrance to our project if the boatmen hadn't been affected. Then it was my turn. Lupi, who had just left the hospital, had to go back in, as well as a bunch of conmen who took advantage of the situation to be sent to the hospital instead of the sick. Gianini and I had firsthand experience of this, being the two sickest of all who showed up at the exam. Many who were not sick at all were admitted to the hospital while Gianini and I were not considered sick. Neither he nor I could stand up, not even before the Internal Service where we were brought after the visit.

The boss guard, less stupid and more human than the Major, sent us to lie down in the cabin. We stayed like that for five days without care. Fortunately we were able to get some medicine and a little milk for ourselves.

During these five days something happened in the camp that we were not expecting, considering the flu epidemic that was ravaging the Islands. There was a convoy of fifty or a hundred men (I don't remember exactly) for Cayenne, and Todd's name was on the list. This was a great surprise to everyone (except him, no doubt). I took advantage of the moment to get the ring out from its hiding place, with great difficulty, and I gave it back to Todd.

"And my stash," he told me, "hurry up, they're coming to get me." It got him all worked up, and me too. I was cooped up, barely able to walk, how was I going to leave?

Who could I resort to? To [Albert] Lévy, who was passing by the cabin. He cost me dearly, but there was no other way. I had him tell Gosset to come get me right away, that I was suffocating in the cabin and would be better off near the crib to get some air. He ran his errand right away and Gosset came to get me. I took advantage of his absence while he was going back and forth to the Internal Service that was shaken up by the convoy. The *Cappy*, which had to transport the men, was expected any minute.

I had a lot of trouble digging it up, not having the strength to use the axe well, and I ended up hitting the stash and damaging it a little. Todd was very annoyed at this accident and I was too. But I alone knew the trouble I had taken keeping it for him and I felt relieved to get rid of the responsibility.

I went back to lie down on the grass near the cowshed. Too sick to move, I didn't see Todd when he departed. He left two hundred francs with Sevox for the two of us.

It was agreed that I would see the boatmen to reach an understanding with them. Alas! What deception! None of them wanted to take the chance anymore, saying that they knew that there would be many convoys and that they would leave for the mainland.

I tried to make them understand that given their situation as boatmen and the free hand they had, they would never have as good an opportunity on the continent. "And if you don't try now, it's because you're greedy; for you freedom is only secondary. You accepted only because Todd promised you five hundred francs when we landed. We only have two hundred to buy provisions and a little for landing. It's yours if you want it."

"No, Duval, not now."

"So when? The sail's going to rot."

"Oh well."

(The sail was found again two years later. An escape attempt had leaked out to the Internal Service, so they searched the dock and even though they saw that it had been hidden a long time before—it was rotten and gone to rags—it still served as incriminating evidence to punish the accused.)

I let the interested parties in on my meeting with the boatmen. Everyone was upset at their response—another thwarted hope. I gave the money back to Sevox, who was reasonable enough not to gamble since he, too, hoped to leave for the mainland. He succeeded in going to Cayenne not by a convoy, but as a witness. A guy named Demangeot had stabbed another convict, whose name I do not remember, a marble worker—it was a matter of pederasty. Demangeot was sentenced to a year in prison and came back to the Islands along with the marble worker. Sevox remained in Cayenne and escaped. Did he succeed? Did he drown? We never had any news.

Later the boatmen were also sent to Cayenne. The Breton escaped and managed to land in Georgetown where he died from a fever he contracted before leaving. His comrades were turned in and came to the Salvation Islands to serve three and five years of imprisonment.

Todd tried to escape under good conditions. A freedman hid him at his house and got some clothes for him. Decked out like a gentleman he was supposed to catch a mail transport, which he would have done if he hadn't been betrayed. By whom? No doubt by those whom he had paid handsomely to help him. He was so well dressed, so well spruced up that they hesitated to arrest him and being scared of making a mistake they were overly polite to the convict. But when he was recognized, he was, of course, no longer a man and their politeness changed into insults and obscenities.

In prison he became friends with the convict Couot, a man who lacked no energy in his escape attempts and who failed in spite of all his courage and boldness. He was very dignified in adversity and never let himself be imposed upon or insulted by his torturers.

I was able to observe him when he came to the Islands: being together in the stone cabin, Girier and I talked with him a lot. He loved this and since he read a lot in his years in prison before being sent to the penal colony, these discussions were sometimes very interesting. But Girier pushed him to the wall. It did not take long to see that he was only superficial, with no grounds for his reasoning. This enraged him and he wanted to hold it against us, especially against Girier who embarrassed him every time. But he was too fond of talking to stay quiet and always began again. He brooded over it and every time came back with a new argument that did not take long to demolish. This did not prevent us from keeping on good terms and being good comrades.

Girier was struck down again by fevers and returned to the infirmary, not to the hospital, oh no, although he needed it. During this time a new convict came to the stone cabin, with a Polish name, Susorski, if I remember correctly. He said he was a schoolteacher from a small French commune and had been sentenced to twenty years of hard labor for aggravated theft. He was a talker whose knowledge (although a school teacher as he called it) was so limited that he talked nonsense that was as crude as it was extravagant, feeble, and trifling. He talked with Couot. The latter almost always pushed him to the wall. But so strongly did he feel the need to talk that he pestered Couot and the discussions began again.

I never took part in this. But one day when he went headlong against the anarchists, insulted them all in general and Ravachol in particular, I went to find him and asked him if he really knew what he was talking about and if he had known Ravachol to speak about him like that.

"No," he told me, "but I know."

"You know what? You know nothing and you only repeat the insults and slanders of a corrupt, sordid press that is so dirty that it tries to dirty everything that is clean, noble, and generous by slobbering on it and spitting its venom like it's always done against men with ideas ahead of their time, valiant pioneers, full of the spirit of justice, who fought for a better quality of life for themselves and their fellow men who were cowardly and spineless just like they are today. That's why the struggle continues and will not stop until the day when a human society will reign where human beings will be truly free and happy, which we are still far from today, unfortunately. And it's you, Mister Convict, who is the victim of a defective social order because if you were a free man, satisfying your needs, you would not be here now in this hell. It's you who get away with insulting those who are fighting for their and your emancipation. It's you who fight against a man who for this reason just put his head in the guillotine. Know that I will not let this just and good-hearted man, this rebel whom we should all imitate, be insulted or slandered by anyone. And also, if you still stand by such words against me and the anarchists, I will smash your head in with a stick from this hammock. When I first got here I almost did it to an imbecile, an idiot like you who insulted the good, valiant woman Louise Michel, whom he did not know. When I told him about her, he changed his mind and said he had only repeated what he'd read in the Catholic newspapers *La Croix* and *Le Pèlerin*. I urge you to do the same, to recognize your mistake or at least to have enough sense to stay quiet. You, a defeated man, disinherited, despoiled, crushed in life, having only duties and no rights."

He considered what I said to him and never had anything more to say on the matter. As a result he became almost an adept of me and Girier.

A foreman had heard what I had said and made a report to the Internal Service who summoned me in order to reprimand me and say that they would not let me make anarchist propaganda like that in the cabins or defend Ravachol.

"I did not defend Ravachol, the environment here is not right for it. I only said that I wouldn't let him be insulted in my presence by anyone."

"Okay, go back to your cabin and control yourself."

Sergeant Raymond left with me and said, "Come on, Duval, be reasonable, put all that aside, think of your wife who you can see again someday if you behave yourself. It's been a long time since you were punished, you'll soon go up to second class, then first and be granted concessions and you will see again the one you love so much. See, all's not lost."

"Certainly, Mr. Raymond, I would be happy to see my dearly beloved again for whom I accept such a miserable existence. But know that despite this I will never be so cowardly as to let anyone insult the comrades who fight for the ideal that is dear to me and that sustains me in this hell as much as my love for my companion does."

"Okay, let's go, Duval, but don't get carried away, don't yell like you did just then. You'll get punished. Go on, get in."

He motioned to the foreman to open the door for me. Everyone was happy to see me, Susorski most of all, thinking that because of our discussion he was the reason I was going to be put in the cell.

## CLEMENTE DUVAL

Line drawing of Clément Duval from the 1930 edition of
his memoirs, *Memorie autobiografiche*. Anarchist Archives
Project, Cambridge, MA.

The anarchist Clément Duval, sentenced to death by the Paris criminal court, January 12, 1887. Sketch in *Le Voleur*, n. 1544, Paris, Feb. 3, 1887.

Cour d'assises de la Seine du 11 et 12 janvier 1887.
Défense (audience du 12 janvier)

Quoique ne vous reconnaissant pas le droit de me poser
les questions et les demandes que vous m'avez faite
je vous ai répondu comme Accusé.

Maintenant c'est en Accusateur

Je ne prétends pas me défendre, — à quoi du reste cela
me servirait — s'il devant des gens aussi bien'armés que vous l'êtes
Ayant Soldats, Canons, Police, et toute une Armée
de Mercenaires, qui se font vos Suppôts.
Soyez logiques, vous êtes la force, profitez en,
Et s'il vous faut encore une Tête D'Anarchiste
prenez la, et le jour de la liquidation on vous en tiendra
compte Et j'ai le ferme espoir que ce jour la les Anarchistes
seront à hauteur de leur mission —

et qu'ils seront sans pitié
Car jamais Ils n'atteindront le nombre de vos Victimes,
Ce n'est pas a vous seuls que je m'adresse,
Mais a la société entière, Cette Société Egoïste
et marâtre, et corrompue où l'on voit d'un Coté l'Orgie,
De l'autre la Misère,
Vous m'inculpez de Vol.
Comme si un travailleur qui ne possède rien,
Que la Misère, peut-être un Voleur — Non !
le Vol n'existe que dans l'exploitation de l'homme —
par l'homme, en un mot de tous ceux qui Vivent
aux dépens de la Classe Productrice.

Duval's defense at his trial, Paris, January 1887.
Handwritten copy by Clément Duval. Archives Nationales
d'outre-mer, Aix-en-Provence.

Fernand Labori, Duval's lawyer. Sketch by Aristide Delannoy in *Les Hommes du Jour*, n. 71, Paris, 1909. CIRA Lausanne.

Les deux derniers convois avaient amenés des Camarades.
Lejeune, Pardaine, Simon, Chérivet, Faugous. Kervaux.
Ce dernier, un sympathique, a qui les Camarades avaient faient
de la propagande pendant la traversée. surtout Simon, qu'il
tenait en haute estime, le voyant si jeune, et si sincère, si
Convaincu.
      Les travaux, pour la Construction de la Réclusion, à
l'Ile St Joseph était Commencés, les nouveaux arrivants débarquèrent
dans cet Ile. Ce qui, a mon grand regret m'empêche de les voir, d'avoir
des nouvelles de France, de la propagande, ce dont j'étais avide.
      Le premier Camarade a qui je serrais les mains.
fut notre malheureux Camarade Girier Lorion, dont a la page
200. du livre "Souvenirs du Bagne" Liard Courtois, raconte
l'arrestation, tel que Girier me l'a raconté lui même.
Inutile, de revenir sur ce sujet. Mais, soit dit en passant.
Nous n'aurons jamais assez de dégoût de mépris, de haine Contre
Deloré. et de tous Ceux qui ont Contribué à l'arrestation de notre
regretté Camarade. traité de mouchard, par de Lâches, et ineptes
                                                        ambitieux.

Manuscript of the memoirs, extract from page 285. CIRA
Lausanne.

Clément Duval at his desk, Brooklyn, NY, around 1930.
CIRA Lausanne.

Clément Duval and friends, Brooklyn, NY, around 1930.
CIRA Lausanne.

# Chapter 7
# Spreading the Good Word

The deportee Boucher, an escape partner of [Vittorio] Pini in Maroni, was sent to the Islands and told me about the escape. He said that Pini had found refuge in Paramaribo with a planter who had accepted money from him and who then was supposed to help him catch a mail transport. But some degenerate escapees who had taken refuge in Paramaribo tried to pass some counterfeit money and caused a manhunt for the escapees who were everywhere in the plantations. Pini ran away to hide and was seen by some police who shot at him. A bullet hit him in the right leg. They picked him up and sent him with all the others to the penitentiary in Maroni and since then he has been in Cayenne waiting to appear before the special Maritime Court.

But he did not know the final details. Girier had told me about the escape of Pini, whom he knew slightly. He was employed as a secretary by the administration officer and Pini was at the chores so they did not see each other much and would never see each other again, since Pini escaped very shortly after Girier's arrival in Maroni. Nevertheless he had good memories of Pini and highly respected him. I had proof of this on January 1, 1893, a rest day. We were shut up in the stone cabin when around two o'clock the *Cappy* arrived from Cayenne. They came to get some chore men to unload the provisions and stuff for the Salvation Islands.

A half hour later our door opened to let a man through and closed again right away. I looked at the poor man, strong, a sound constitution but pale and anemic, with a shifty look, hardened by physical and moral suffering. I felt attracted by his tan face with energetic traits. Girier, who was busy sewing, mending some pants, looked up and said to me, "But that's Pini!"

Right away he jumped off the hammock and went to shake his hand. I did the same. Both of us wanted to shake the hand of a comrade and embrace him, but even though he experienced the same joy as we did at shaking the hands of friends, even though he was betrayed by his emotion, we felt like he was colder, less exuberant and less communicative, at least for the moment. We helped him set up his hammock and seeing that he was unwell we put him to bed and gave him the information he asked us for in order to see the doctor because he needed to go to the hospital to take care of the diarrhea that had been wearing him down for more than a year.

❊ ❊ ❊

The following day he went to the doctor and was admitted to the hospital. At the bottom of the stairs he met a convict from the convoy, Roulier, who was sentenced, I think, to twelve years of hard labor for falsification of accounts at the Samaritaine [Paris department store]. He had been sent to Kourou or to Cayenne and then came to the Islands and did some secretary work for the Internal Service, which earned him the C.M. [contremaître, the foreman's insignia] on his arm. I don't know how he could have accepted this executioner's work as a foreman because he was really not made for it.

Shaking Pini's hand he expressed his regrets at having been sent to the Islands. "Where, of course, you are also interned. But you have some comfort—to find yourself with friends who share your ideas and maybe trust is strength. Duval has tried to escape many times, maybe the two of you will be able to succeed. And I assure you that even though I have the C.M. on my arm (which might make you distrust me) I won't be the one to put a snag in your plans. It's just the opposite, because even if I don't share your ideas, I think they're grand and that whoever fights for their fulfillment doesn't deserve to be here."

Pini told me about this conversation when he got out of the hospital.

But on the same day Roulier told me Pini's response, which upset me a lot. He responded, "I don't know Duval and I have nothing to do with him. If I get a little better and you can help me, I'll be off this rock in six months."

This dear, late comrade had not yet acquired enough experience in the penal colony. He was going to become an apprentice. With his honest and loyal nature, cruel deceptions were awaiting him in that bleak environment.

He stayed around a month in the hospital on a milk diet, but no longer able to consume the condensed milk they were giving him and dying of hunger, he asked to leave. When he came back to the stone cabin I gently criticized him for his response to Roulier that really bothered me. He took both my hands and said that it was just to put them off the track and he urged me to talk with him as little as possible, only when it was necessary to do so about our plans. That way we wouldn't raise any suspicions.

"My dear Pini, I know the penal colony better than you. I learned at my own expense. I assure you that acting like that is not the way to go and it will end up backfiring on us. You must understand that you're going to be under special surveillance just like me and all the other comrades, but a little less than us since you haven't tried to escape from here yet. Therefore, for the administration, knowing that we have common ideas, it's no surprise that we hang out together and that we're good friends. Whereas if we don't talk except now and again when we need to, we will look much more suspicious."

Girier, who was present at this conversation, said I was right. Pini made no objection. And from then on all three of us ate together. Neither of them could eat the rancid bacon and stew, so every day I made a bread soup for the three of us. Sometimes I got some lettuce leaves and potatoes and made some spinach—a day like that was a gala feast.

Sometimes when I made some stuff for a guard's wife or the nuns who gave me a pan to repair or something, instead of a pack of tobacco or a glass of wine I asked for some potatoes so I could fix a ragout on meat days. On these days the lechers and parasites dining at the Grand Hotel did not find their meals as succulent as we did with simple potatoes that they would have turned their noses up at and thrown in the face of any intruder who tried to serve such a dish.

(This brings something to mind, showing me what our poor humanity is: man has tamed himself more than all the animals, which might snap at or snatch away the food that they are refused. But man is still satisfied with a bone to chew on from time to time. A veritable wreck who accepts the little reforms that they surrender to him when he bares his teeth just slightly. Damn! When will he bite them for good in order to be free and happy?)

With this small change in diet, Girier and Pini got a little better. The latter felt strong enough to have a go at something and asked me if it was possible to get a dinghy from the dock.

"With energy and boldness it can be done. I've tried it several times." And I told him how I failed every time and had abandoned the idea. "But being two men who trust each other, which is a strength, maybe strong enough to spur on someone hesitating at the right moment, we are going to try again."

Alas, for the same reasons as was told above this attempt failed and weakened Pini's health so that he was put in the infirmary. Girier's fevers came back and he had to go back there again too. Faugoux, who got sick on Saint Joseph Island, was left with no care. The diarrhea that he had contracted because of the change in climate, overwork, and bad food got worse. Instead of sending him to the hospital where he would have had some care, they put him in the infirmary where there was nothing but a little quinine, bismuth, and food like in the camp. So he stayed there three weeks, left in the same condition, and was sent to Saint Joseph to be used on the pick and shovel and to roll huge blocks of stone, for which he did not have the strength.

Every evening before the roll call I took advantage of the fact that the door stayed open to go and see these comrades and I talked with Faugoux whom I was able to appreciate as being truly, in every respect, a good, energetic, courageous comrade. Also, like everyone who knew him I highly respected him and was really upset to see him in such a condition, feeling that there was some prejudice, that they were not giving him the care that his condition required and that his sickness was killing him.

We talked about comrade Cails, whom he knew very well and respected, but was sorry that he did not react against his impulsive nature that could drag him into a catastrophe whose consequences he did not evaluate concerning the result for propaganda. He was not wrong: later Cails was caught in a trap set by the police in London. His upright nature was not able to imagine such an infamous plot, so he was caught, which cost him ten years of hard labor that he did in England.

Comrade Chevenet, sentenced like Faugoux for the ammunition in Soisy-sous-Étiolles, fell ill, but was luckier than the latter. He was cared for right away at the hospital where he stayed for a month, during which time I saw him a few times. He told me that the comrades on Saint Joseph were fed up with this life and did not want to die like this.

"Couldn't there be some way to try to take over by force? Too bad if we pay with our lives. There's a convict on Saint Joseph, an intelligent guy, named Plista, who will march with us. What do you think, Duval, since you know the Islands better than we do? How should we go about it?"

"Comrade, I'm glad to hear you speaking like that and to learn that the comrades on Saint Joseph are feeling the same way and are on our side. I've spoken about this with Pini and we came up with a plan that might be feasible if all the comrades on Saint Joseph are concentrated on Royal Island with the other men I know we can count on. We will be able to try a takeover with a chance of success. We'll see; it's not possible right now because I'm afraid it won't be easy to join together here. Tell our comrades that our intentions are the same as theirs, but to be patient in order to see it through. According to the newspapers that we've been able to see, we've found out that several comrades have been sent up. They'll be here soon and there are even some already on their way who will here in a few days on the next convoy."

"Ah, comrade Duval, all the comrades on Saint Joseph are going to be very glad to hear this news! It'll raise their spirits again. Little Simon, who's got a restless nature, can't put up with this life and says rightly that we're cowards to accept it. I'm going to urge him not to yell this out in the cabins like he does so that nothing regrettable happen to him."

"You're right, comrade Chevenet, we shouldn't waste our energy for nothing, I mean just for words. If one of us is put in the cell, it'll mean one less man on the day of action, so patience and discretion above all else. Do you know this Plista very well who you told me about?"

"Oh, yes! He's full of energy and all of us have total confidence in him."

"It could be, my friend, that your trust is well placed, but nevertheless, be careful with those who don't share our ideas, who aren't comrades. How long is his sentence and for what?"

"I think he's sentenced to twenty years, but I don't know why. I'll find out. Anyway it's not for anarchy. He himself admits he's never had anything do with it, except that today he's met some anarchists and they're not bad, vicious, unruly men like the press makes them out to be, but on the contrary they're good, selfless men prepared to sacrifice their lives to demand their rights. Anyway, you'll see him, he'll probably be coming to the hospital because he's sick too and doesn't want to die here. That's why he wants to act as quickly as possible. We often speak about the comrades on Royal Island, so he'll be happy to meet you."

"That's good, I'll see him. Since we're not ready yet, don't tell him about our plans and make sure the other convicts do the same."

"You can count on my discretion, Duval. It's too serious not to keep it secret, even with respect to Plista who, I think, will be with us when it's time to act."

We left each other and I didn't see Chevenet again until the day he left the hospital. Unfortunately, I only had time to shake his hand and tell him to give my regards to the comrades on Saint Joseph.

Louise Michel said somewhere that it may well be that premonition is a sixth sense, so often do those things happen that we have a premonition about. Such was the case with Plista, whom I did not know and in whom I had no trust, sensing in him a coward and a traitor. Events proved me right.

I reported our conversation to Pini and Girier, who didn't share our enthusiasm and told us, "The plan is great for comrades in your situation. But I'm young and have a relatively short sentence compared with you and if the sickness doesn't do me in, I feel strong enough to serve it out and when I'm free I'll stay in the colony, do some farming, and expose the negligence of the administration. I'll take the opportunity to make some active propaganda. There's work to do here just like everywhere else and I'll devote myself to it entirely."

We felt the apostle in these words, as well as in his answers to the objections we made to him about the obstacles he would face and their consequences.

"I thought about all that, but with the experience I've acquired here, they won't take me down as easily as you think. Since I'll be freed, I will certainly have the chance to evade them. But I'll be in Guiana for life—if I return to France, I won't be able to do anything, I'll be hunted down like a wild beast for going back illegally. In any other country what good would I be for propaganda? Whereas here there's so much need to spread the good word in order to destroy the fetishism and ignorance and all that. And of course I won't be alone, our good comrade Lepiez and I will be freed almost at the same time, then Paridaën and others will follow. We'll be a force. And you, Duval, if you don't manage to escape, you can be granted concessions around the same time, maybe even before. And if your companion comes to join you like she wants, we'll be a little band that will know how to respect one another and make ourselves known like you have done all by yourself, drawing your strength from logic and the sincerity of your convictions. We'll do the same and, believe me, our efforts will not be in vain, they will be felt all the way to France where there are friends who will help us to bring our propaganda to fruition. Ah! I'm not kidding myself, the work is hard. We have to take out of their brains all the prejudices, errors, and fanaticism that the missionaries have ingrained among the people. By our conduct we can make ourselves loved by this population that will come to us, listen to us, and later be our defenders against enemies and persecutors. This will be a fight to the death because we'll go all the way and if we fall, it will be by their bullets and not in their cabins. We'll never come back to this hell, where I hope you will leave right away, my good friends, and for this I want with all my heart for your plan to succeed."

Thus our late Girier spoke to Pini and me.

Pini responded, "You're free to act like that and we don't blame you. We also want you to succeed. As for me, I would like to leave this country as fast as I can. Since we can't act right now, I'll take advantage of the slightest opportunity to get out of here as soon as possible."

And that we did not hesitate to try.

After he left the infirmary Pini was employed as a gardener behind the cowshed. Being close to each other, we began preparations for our escape on a raft that we wanted to take under favorable conditions in order not to have to dock on the continent right away and get picked up. But they did not give us time. Suspecting or noticing something, the Interior Service took Pini out of the garden and put him in front of the Service so they could watch him, like me, more closely.

Pini suffered from that diarrhea that dogged him, had to return to the doctor, and was put back in the infirmary where he got hooked up with a guy named Poitoux, whom he had known in Maroni, and along with Buenerd, who was also suffering, was in the infirmary where there was a nurse named Costa. All three noticed that there were beams under the infirmary and various things that could be used to make a raft. With what they could get from outside, they decided to take a chance. For that it was absolutely necessary to fill Costa in on the escape plan and Pini had him come to get me. Costa accepted and came to let me know what Pini wanted me to get for him.

"Okay," I said to him, "tell Pini that I'll see him after the doctor's visit."

I criticized him for confiding in Costa, who did not deserve such trust.

"It was impossible to do otherwise."

"And how well do you know Poitoux?"

"I knew him a little in Maroni."

"Yes, but maybe not well enough for this plan. My dear Pini, let me tell you that all three of you are going to act stupidly if you leave like this, being sick and all. At least get a little better. None of you can even stand up straight. An escape under these conditions is suicide, even if you manage to reach the continent. It would be wiser to wait and put our plan into execution for which you and Buenerd are two indispensable units."

"Too bad. It's an opportunity here. We're going to take it and leave this evening, as soon as night falls. So, everything has to be prepared during the siesta, I'm counting on you, Duval, to bring me the stuff I need that you've got in your tool crib."

"Pini, you're upsetting me because I can see the outcome. But I don't want you to criticize me (in spite of the fact that it would be for your own good) for something I can get for you and that you need. I'll give you what you ask for. But not before one o'clock when they start working again and I hand out the tools to the men on chores."

"No, no, we need it in two hours. Poitoux will go down under the infirmary during the siesta—that's the only good time for us to prepare."

"I'm sorry, but that's impossible. I know the guard on duty at that time. He's a rat who's always hanging around the stone cabin and the infirmary. If he sees me, all is lost for you and I'll be put in the cell. And for you to leave and come get them is also impossible. Plus, I have a premonition. Does Costa know it's for tonight?"

"Yes."

"Okay. I won't be at all surprised if they search the infirmary during the siesta. This guard loves to annoy the men with searches. What will be taken as one of his vicious fantasies, which are so common, will, maybe, be nothing but Costa's informing. Watch out."

"That's impossible, he's too involved with us."

"Can you prove that?"

"No, and even if I could, I wouldn't."

"I know it, Pini, and he knows it too. Believe me, let it go for now and make everything that can incriminate you disappear."

"Ah, no! An opportunity like this to have beams that float won't come again. And all the trouble that we've taken? But since you don't want to give us what we've asked you for, we'll do without it."

He left in a fit. I was so upset that I was on the point of bringing the stuff to him. But the premonition and my rationality prevented me, very fortunately. What I had predicted was happening. At 11:00 a.m. the guard on duty along with by the infirmary guard and two foremen broke into the infirmary and made a search not so much of the men but of the floor under the hammocks, lifting up two planks around Poitoux's and asking him why he had taken the nails out. He denied it, naturally. They searched with a fine-toothed comb, found various little things that seemed suspicious to them and then they opened the door and found the beams, cords, and everything else.

They put Poitoux in the cell. He kept denying it and was only given sixty days of solitary. In the afternoon the Commandant came and made them take away the beams while bawling out the boss guard for leaving such things in reach of the convicts.

There was such a commotion in the camp that I couldn't see Pini until the next day. He was not angry anymore and he congratulated me on not giving in to his demands and he said that he should have listened to me since I had more experience than him of the penitentiary and of men.

"Yes, like you I have learned at my own expense."

Poitoux behaved honorably in the matter. When we could we slipped him some bread and tobacco.

Pini left the infirmary and they put him with two others planting coconut trees. These two wretched characters took advantage of Pini's conscientious work (like we should do when we accept it or have the courage to refuse) so that they did nothing, even in spite of the reproaches of the field guard who told off all three.

Pini said to the two of them, "Work a little so you won't be told off and humiliated like that or just refuse outright."

"Ah!" they said, "and now the anarchist is asking us to work. Work yourself if you want, we want to do nothing."

"Don't tell me that, tell the guard. But you're too cowardly for that. When he's here, you'll tell him that you did all the work."

If it were not for the chore, the argument would have degenerated into a brawl.

That evening Pini told us about it. The outrage hurt him. He went to the doctor and was admitted to the hospital.

❊ ❊ ❊

When Major Crossaire came to the Islands to replace Major Liatta, Gosset was ordered by the Interior Service to get some men on chores to take the Major's baggage. The work should have stopped there, but he overdid it and had them arrange the furniture and he kept asking the Major's wife, "Where would you like to put this, Madam? How would you like that set up?"

It got so bad that when the drum beat for the end of work the men on chores, seeing that they were nowhere near finishing, left Gosset alone. The following day he complained to me, telling me that they deserved to be punished.

"They told me what happened. You didn't offer to give them anything to thank them for the extra work that you were making them do. They acted rightly. If I had been in their place I would have left much sooner and if you get them punished I'll think you are the worst swine of all."

"Hey, calm down, Duval, I won't do it. But if you knew how nice, sweet, and lovable the Major's wife is!"

I realized afterward that, in fact, the qualities of this lady had charmed him to the point that he neglected to watch me as he had been ordered. He spent part of his day with her, happy to be of any use. This worked in my favor for the escape that Pini, Buenerd, and I wanted to attempt. It gave me the opportunity to prepare what we needed.

This deserves a short digression.

A little before I left the construction workshop they began designing a new workshop located near the wells in the north. They began by taking away everything that was stored under the transportation hospital: pump, materials, hardware, etc. When nothing was left I returned the keys to the works guard. But before that, I took apart the lock and installed what in locksmith's terms is called a spike, which consists of fastening a little round or flat iron piece to prevent the key from entering. I notched one key to bypass the spike and thus found myself with the only key that could open the door, thinking this might come in handy one day. As we will see later, it did.

Major Crossaire did not want to ask anything from the different services, at least not to be completely committed to them, so he asked Gosset if he knew a convict to fix the locks in his apartment, which weren't working well, and the doorbell as well. Gosset gave him my name.

The Major grimaced, "But you're offering me an anarchist!"

"Yes, but you'll have no complaints about him, I'm sure."

"Will I have to ask the Internal Service?"

"No, he works with me to repair the service's tools. I'll tell them and they'll give him to you for the work."

"Okay, he can come tomorrow after the siesta, around 1:30."

When Gosset let me in on this I was not very happy and grumbled about it, telling him that he was not in a position to give my word like that and he should at least have consulted me beforehand. "But in the end, I'll go tomorrow."

After crossing the garden I found the Major in a lounge chair on the veranda. He told me to wait a little while because the Mrs. was resting with their daughter. Then he told me what he wanted.

"No problem, Major, I'll take apart the locks and see what's wrong. I think there's probably no damage. They simply need to be cleaned and greased."

"There should have been someone from the works service for this maintenance."

"Yes, but I think that this service, like all the others in the administration, leaves much to be desired—and the medical service is no better."

"Ah, okay, good, you're not afraid to say what you think. Yet, in your situation it's a little risky. I know some colleagues who wouldn't put up with such an answer and would stick you in a cell."

"Those gentlemen would have a lot more to complain about than me because it would demonstrate very bad manners for educated men."

"Ah, I see very clearly that you're an anarchist! Are there many like you here?"

"A few. Among others there's one whom I highly respect who's in your service and very sick."

"What's he got?"

"Chronic diarrhea, really exhausting."

"What's his name?"

"Pini."

"I think I know the name, I'll see."

We continued to discuss anarchy for half an hour. Then his wife got up and I went up his rooms.

Should I tell how I felt at the sight of this sweet, kind, beautiful woman?

Yes, since these lines are impressions, sensations of a life lived and this was the only sensation of the kind that I experienced during my stay in that hell. I was in contact with many of the guards' wives to make stuff for them and also when they needed work done on their houses and I found many of them to be kind and beautiful. But the image of my companion was so deeply engraved in my heart that she was continually reflected before my eyes. I never desired another woman but her. It was not the same with the Major's wife for whom I felt a desire so much more passionate considering the seven-year deprivation of a natural need. I was there for three afternoons to do the work. I was very happy when I arrived and leaving made me sad. I dreamed of her during the night, heard that sweet voice talking to me just as it did during the day, very freely and very considerately so as not to make me feel my place as a convict. When I finished she gave me five francs and a bottle of wine, telling me that she was very satisfied and that if they needed something again, they would ask me. I never went back, but I saw her sometimes on the road, walking with her young daughter. Each time she said hello to me without haughtiness and smiled kindly. She was really a good person, good for the convicts.

For his part, the Major spoke with Pini and got him some good treatment, which helped to get him back on his feet for a little while for a new escape attempt. It was agreed that I would prepare everything I could and we would get the rest with the money Todd had left me—seventy francs, plus a dozen or so that Buenerd had and ten more that I had earned, a total of ninety francs—a fortune under the circumstances.

We were shown once again how this vile metal is the great social wound and corrupts individuals who will risk everything (the cell, bullets) for a coin worth a hundred sous, ten francs. They would not have done anything out of friendship. They were completely indifferent to comrades in misfortune, even to themselves, most of them. But the attraction of a coin, which they were going to lose gambling or get taken away by a slave driver with thirty or sixty days' punishment in the cell, gave them courage and boldness.

No doubt it was dangerous to bring me the requested material so I could hide it under the transportation hospital, to which I had the key. And then it was necessary to be cautious in the choice of individuals in order not to be betrayed by them. Fortunately, there were some who were in a good position to help us and from whom we had nothing to fear.

We bought sheets from a nurse and Pini took charge of making the sail because we wanted to make a raft not simply to reach the continent, but to lead us to a good harbor, which would take a little while, but not too much. We had provisions accordingly. In the storeroom for the old things of the dead, I got two changes of clothes for each of us in the blue cloth of freedmen, almost new. Finally at the end of a month everything was ready. We had overcome all the obstacles.

Our departure should have taken place on a Sunday at nightfall when it was bedtime. If we could make the two trips with no hitches to take the material to the seashore, our raft would be ready, we could get on quickly and get out of there. We went to bed Saturday night with this hope in mind.

And so I was very surprised when after the roll call on Sunday morning they made all the men go back in their squads instead of taking them to wash and bathe and Gosset didn't come to get me like I had asked him to.

Then a commotion arose in the camp, which was strange. Everyone was wondering what could be going on. It was only at 2:00 p.m. that we got word of the mystery when we saw the Commandant and the boss guard along with five or six foremen, one of whom was Gosset. After searching everywhere they stopped in front of the door leading under the hospital. When the works guard could not open it, he sent for the guy who had replaced me. Unable to open the door they broke it down and everything was discovered and brought to the Internal Service.

The Commandant and the rest passed by the stone cabin, looking satisfied with their discovery. It was not the same for us since we figured that we'd been betrayed. I waited to see them open the door at any minute to take me to the cell. Since Pini and Buenerd were hospitalized, it would wait for the next day.

Around 3:30 Gosset came to get me. I said to myself, "There you go."

But he was very nice and said, "Don't hold it against me, Duval, if I didn't come to get you earlier, it's because of that imbecile Prat."

I understood nothing of this so I hurried to get to the crib so he could explain it to me. He informed me that Prat was in the holding cell for breaking into the room of the hospital guard and stealing money from the guard Genais who was living with him at the time. He got sick in the cell and the doctor who made the visit sent him to the hospital. Then, yesterday evening he was reported missing on the first round by the guard who was with the Sister. They searched everywhere, but found nothing. This morning at the break of day, on the seashore, at the Flat Rock, they found a jacket and pants with his number and a written note: "Being sentenced to life and in custody for theft, which will cost me another punishment in solitary that will be a slow death in this tomb, I'd rather just die right now. That's why

I'm committing suicide. I ask forgiveness for the wrongs I've done. My final farewells to those whom I loved. Prat."

When they brought this note to the boss guard, he said, "So much the better for him if it's true, it's the best thing to do. But I knew this lowlife, it's probably just to put us off his scent."

He ordered them to continue the search and at noon they found Prat up in a coconut tree. He was taken to the cell, sheepish and in a sorry state. Under harsh interrogation he admitted that he didn't have the courage to kill himself, as he intended, and so he hid in the coconut tree. When they asked him why he didn't give himself up to the Internal Service, which would have made his case less serious, since now he was guilty of attempted escape as well, "Because you wanted to escape, didn't you?"

"No," he answered.

That is all they could get out of him.

The Commandant went to the Internal Service and asked the boss guard if he had discovered any clues to prove he was trying to escape.

"No, Commandant," the boss guard answered.

"Have you searched everywhere carefully?"

"Yes, Commandant."

"Under the hospital?"

"No, they checked that everything was shipshape, the door was firmly shut by the works men who took everything away, tools, materials and all."

"Okay," said the Commandant, "show me where you found Prat's clothes and note."

They went down to the seashore and made a trip around the hospital. The Commandant noticed that where they wash the dishes there were some boards on the floor that had been put back in place and were easy to unfasten. He sent for the machinist guard, showed it to him and when they passed by the door he had the bad (for us) idea to get it opened. That's how they discovered what we had taken so much trouble to get and hide.

When Gosset finished telling me the story in all its details, which were very important to me, I was glad to know that there had been no betrayal—it somewhat alleviated the pain I felt. Only, I racked my brain trying to find out why Prat had acted like that. Was it just a bad break that he wanted to commit suicide? The suicide coincided with our escape attempt—that was really rotten luck.

I had to wait for the next day to give the information to Pini. In the meantime Gosset said to me, "I have the same opinion as the Commandant, who told me that it was some cagey fellows who had made the preparations."

Then looking at me and laughing, "And you're not unfamiliar with that, are you?"

"So tell me, Gosset, what makes you think that?"

"It's not a thought, there's proof. But calm down, I won't say anything."

"What proof?"

"Six pairs of pants and six freedmen jackets coming from the storeroom whose key I have and different things that I recognized as yours, since I saw you make them here. I thought it was just stuff you were making to earn some change, so I didn't pay attention. Now my opinion is that you wanted to escape with Pini."

"You're wrong and even if it were so, what does it have to do with you? You're a convict like me, a slave like me, captive in this hell and far from those who are dear to you and who love you. There's only one difference—our morality. If, as you think, I were one of the planners of this escape attempt, it would prove that I had the courage to try to get myself out of this slavery, this captivity. Meanwhile you're a zealous slave and the flunky of your slave drivers, your executioners—ugh! You said just now that I had nothing to fear and you wouldn't betray me. But if that's true, it's in your interest to stay quiet because they'll tell you, 'What? You're responsible for watching Duval and before your very eyes you let him make these things he was bound to use for an escape? You're responsible for the storeroom of old clothes and you let him take six pairs of pants and six jackets. If you were his accomplice, you wouldn't have acted any differently.' That's what they will say to you, my friend. As you see, you only have to keep your mouth shut if you don't want this to come down on your head."

He understood this and I knew he understood.

The next day, at the risk of getting myself punished, when the medical visit had barely finished, I went to find Pini to see what he knew about Prat, who had been in the same room with him. I was surprised to find him in such a (you would almost say moribund) state.

"What's wrong, Pini? Are you getting sicker?"

"Oh, my friend," he said to me, "I had a horrible night. What happened to us is my fault."

"How's that? Anyway, it's no reason to get alarmed like this. It can only worsen your condition, which is getting better, even much better."

"Be careful, Duval, it's a bad time to be talking. The guards can come in at any minute. Come back later and I'll tell you what's up."

"No, Pini, I'll come tomorrow. For today, take a rest."

"No, no, it'll bring me some relief to tell you the stupid thing I did and the shameful way Prat deceived me."

Around 2:30, at the time I was getting ready to go to see Pini, (Gosset had left early), I was called to the Internal Service and the guard Raymond went with me to see the Commandant. On the way I asked him why.

"I don't know," he said.

When I showed up in front of the Commandant, he seemed to be in a good mood because it was in a good-natured, almost happy voice that he said to me, "Come on, Duval, you're always going to be incorrigible when it comes to escaping. Once again you wanted to fly the coop. If it weren't for Prat it would've been a nice little trick. You were leaving with Pini, weren't you? It's good for me that once again luck was not on your side. Otherwise I would have been fired for letting two boys like you escape, you who are considered very dangerous and therefore the object of special surveillance. As for calling you dangerous, I know you too well to attach any importance to it except as a rebel against the establishment, against things sanctioned by the law. And all your comrades who are here are the same, aren't they?"

"Yes, Commandant."

"And for that you're all dangerous. That's why, since my responsibility is greater toward the anarchists than the other convicts, the flight of one of you would surely get me fired, which you don't care about, seeing that you just tried to escape again with Pini. You won't deny it, will you?"

"Commandant, you are accusing me of something of which you have no proof."

"No proof? And this?" he asked and he showed me the lock that he took out of a box on the table. "Are you going to deny that it was you who rigged this lock so that we couldn't open the door that you had an extra key for in case you needed to get under the hospital? Congratulations, Duval, the phobia of escaping makes you cautious."

That last was said ironically, but everything was so true that I was dumbfounded. However, to fess up would have been to give in and play into my slave drivers' hands. Since I can't stand denying an action that I wanted to declare out loud, I figured out a way not to say yes or no.

I answered him, "But, Commandant, what proves that it was me who rigged the lock?"

"Because it's been like this only since we moved the equipment and materials from under the hospital. You were part of the works at the time and Genais went to the place every day and the door worked fine. Since there was no need to go back there, we never noticed that the lock had been tampered with. It was lucky that I was inspired to open it. Otherwise Pini, you, and maybe another might have managed to escape. It's true that you wouldn't have got far. We would have caught you, which means that, in short, it's better for you that it turned out this way. Answer frankly, like you usually do. You prepared this escape, everything proves it: the lock and the freedmen clothes taken from the storeroom that Gosset had the key to and that you had taken while he was gone. You see, Duval, all the evidence is enough for me to deal with you harshly. Yet, this time I don't intend to punish you, at least as long as the head office, where I sent the report, doesn't force me to."

"Commandant, it would only be fair, the evidence you're presenting is only circumstantial and not material. What proves that someone else didn't tamper with the lock? What proves that I was the one who took the freedmen clothes?"

He smiled and told the guard to take me back to my work.

At that time Director Vérignon had just left for France and had been replaced by Assistant Director Guégan, who let the Commandant act freely in the matter. That's why Pini and I were not punished. When he made a tour of the penitentiaries he came to the Islands and asked the Commandant if we had been punished.

"No," he answered, "they fooled the guards' vigilance too well, did no harm to the administration and had no intention of making trouble on the continent since they had provisions and everything they needed to get far away. But I'll catch them again when I don't have just circumstantial evidence, but material proof as well. They'll pay for both times then."

"It would be good to do so. We mustn't go easy on these boys."

That's what was reported to me by one the Commandant's employees who had overheard the conversation and many other things, proving that Guégan was a worthy imitator of his boss Vérignon or at least as dishonest and brutal.

The next day I saw Pini and told him about the interrogation. He told me that Prat, a Frenchman, was born in Italy where he stayed until he was twelve years old and he spoke Italian very well. In France he learned the tailor's trade.

"Since he was in my room he saw my comings and goings and he saw us talking together. He smiled and said to me: 'You're not happy on this rock, you really want to leave.' I answered vaguely at first, but then our conversations become more intimate. Prat let me in on his future projects, of his intention to leave the Islands immediately, if it was possible, given his situation counting on a punishment of imprisonment or of solitary and he asked to come with us, that he clearly saw that we were preparing an escape. I know it wasn't true: he had been informed by one of his partners whom we'd used as a go-between and paid cheaply for what he'd offered us. Thinking he was sincere and was about to go before the Council, I took pity on him and told him that there were in fact three of us who were going to leave and that if we could get all the materials we wanted, we could take a fourth and it would be him. He couldn't hold back his joy and shook my hand telling me, 'Thank you, Pini, you won't regret bringing me along. I can be useful because I was kind of a sailor.' 'All the better because the three of us are not. Before that you can still make yourself useful. I'm in charge of making the sail and it's not easy. Someone needs to be on the lookout. Since you're a tailor, you can do the stitching quickly while I keep an eye out so that no one will see you or bother you.' 'It's a deal,' he told me. 'I'll dash it off fast.' In fact, he did do it quickly and when I gave it to you to hide, I didn't have time to tell you this because we were interrupted by the guard's arrival. You know the rest. But why did he leave the hospital for the so-called suicide and hide in a coconut tree? I have no idea and I can't understand it. Oh! My dear Duval," Pini said to me, putting his hands on my shoulders, "I am so sorry for what happened because of me. Today, maybe, we'd be far away from here."

"My dear Pini, there's no use moaning about it or criticizing yourself. What you did was for the best—to save a man in need. The wrong you did was to not talk to me earlier. Buenerd knew Prat enough not to trust him so much. I myself saw him for a few days in the stone cabin looking around to rob his comrades. That's why I didn't like him very much. In this matter there was some crookedness that I, like you, still can't explain, but we know it."

A few days later we found out about his plan. Knowing from Pini that everything was ready and that we were planning to leave on Sunday, he informed two of his partners (little rats like him) and told them that he would leave the hospital on Saturday, pretend to kill himself and hide. The guards would be on the warpath looking for him and we wouldn't be able to leave until later. So, at the end of two or three days, not finding him, they would think that he really did kill himself and his partners could meet him at a predetermined place and they would leave with our stuff, which had been so hard for us to get, at every moment risking the cell, the hole, and even bullets.

It is surprising that we were able to completely escape not only the attention of the guards, but of the asses who swarm on this rock. All of our money had been spent to pull it off right and we failed just because of a lowlife like him (of which there are plenty in this sorry place. See, you find a lot of good men, but also quite a lot of scoundrels, of whom Prat is the perfect example). There was only one thing he did not think of: the door, which was not easy to force open. That's what probably got him caught.

Pini was fuming for having been fooled like that and said to me, "If I could get a hold of Prat, I would crush his skull like the viper he is."

"My friend, calm down, there are plenty of vipers like him here. That's why in the future I urge you to be more cautious. Let's forget about this letdown and add it to all the others we've had and will probably have again. Don't beat yourself up like this. Think of getting back on your feet and figure on finding a doctor who will take care of you, which doesn't always happen, especially for anarchists. I know something about that through personal experience. And let's wait patiently for the arrival of new comrades who, like us, have fallen in the fight, so we can initiate them into this environment so they won't be fooled like us. Thus warned they'll be cautious and we can work safely and soundly as we should."

"You're right, Duval, and it's comforting to know by what you say that you haven't lost hope and still have some confidence."

"That's how I've been able to stand this wretched existence until now. The day when I have no more hope to leave here, I'll sell my skin, and for as much as possible, unless sickness sucks out the necessary energy and prevents me from doing it. Let's go, my dear Pini, we have to leave so they won't find us together. Take care and buck up."

We left each other after a good, strong, friendly handshake.

I saw Pini again two or three times a week and noticed that his health was returning little by little. When he was outside and the moment was right, Girier stopped turning the filter at the water tank, which was near the hospital, and went to shake Pini's hand, to give him a few good words of friendship to comfort him. In the evening in the cabin he told me how he was and the conversation turned back on him and on our comrades in misfortune and on those who were happier still being in the thick of things.

# Chapter 8
# David and Ballin

The new director De Laloyère arrived. He came to the Islands while making a tour of the penitentiaries. [Eugène] Allmayer petitioned him for a job and offered his services to the administration. He took it under consideration and Allmayer was catapulted into the position of bigwig secretary of the infirmary where he could peddle as he wished, to the detriment of the sick. He had his "little wife," the Corporal, working with him as a nurse.

❖ ❖ ❖

Commandant Leboucher replaced the office boss Bravaud. He did not seem any worse than any other, yet under his administration something happened that was as atrocious as anything that can count among the annals of the slave drivers.

The deportees [Eugène] David and [Auguste] Ballin had been sentenced to three years of imprisonment for escaping. The cabin roofs of the personnel and the transportation were in need of total repair or at least restoration and since this was necessary for the administration, they did not hesitate one minute to violate the regulations by employing the two of them in the works as roofers, which was their profession.

David and Ballin figured they were on the rock for at least three years and not sure to leave at the end of their sentence, so decided to make the most of the opportunity that presented itself—to escape if it was possible. They discovered an excavation in the rocks where they could hide the materials to build a little tin dinghy and work on it for a little while every day and when most of the work was done they would not have to go back to prison, they could board their little craft and get away in the night to a more hospitable land.

The baker who had replaced Meurse (gone to Kourou) was to take part in this escape because his cooperation was very useful to them. When I found out that the baker was with them and that Costa the nurse was in on the secret, I lost all faith in their success and let Ballin know it, telling him that the baker was the one who was going to give them up and make the attempt fail, even though he was in on it.

"As for Costa, he's a little blabbermouth whom you can't trust in such serious matters."

"I know it," said Ballin, "but we absolutely need him to get some things. He's already in deep."

"Go on, my friend, good luck and if I can be of any use, it would be my pleasure."

"I know and since I can't see you very often, I'll tell Girier since I see him every night in the prison. He won't betray me, will he? If I weren't tormented by these preparations for the escape, I'd be glad to return to prison in the evening to chat with Girier. He's a good and intelligent man whom I highly respect."

I did not see Ballin again and I always remember the words of this good, courageous, energetic convict concerning our late comrade.

The preparations made good progress and up to this point everything went marvelously. They worked hard to have a moment to themselves every day. In the works they were satisfied and the guard who passed by their construction site three or four times a day congratulated them and gave them a quarter liter of wine now and then or a pack tobacco, which they had no right to since they were being punished.

Now, one Saturday after the guard had passed by their site as usual, they went to their hiding place. At this very moment a note was sent to the works to get the roofers to come to fix the leak in some bureaucrat's roof.

Bad luck called on David and Ballin to be the ones destined to make the repair (because there were other roofers). The foreman who came to fetch them realized that they were not at their site. The guard came after and found no one. Though they were known as being good workers, they were also known as being escape artists. The guard reported to the Internal Service about their disappearance from the construction site. All the foremen and the slave drivers with their bloodhounds were on the move and the manhunt got underway. All the excavations were searched except for theirs, which was obviously not known about.

David and Ballin heard the noise and understood that they were searching for them. If they left their hiding place, they would be led straight to the cell, put in irons, and not get out for work anymore. They decided to stay put, hurry up making their dinghy, and take off during the night if it was finished, counting on the baker to come join them in the night or, if he couldn't come, to wait until the next day.

What a surprise they had to see that during the night the guards and foremen were waiting for them to leave their hiding place, not even trying to search for them. They tried to leave several times, but the dogs were keeping a close watch. They decided to wait for daylight when they would see better to defend themselves and deal with the guns, knowing full well that the guards wouldn't hesitate to murder them. During this time they investigated their excavation and noticed that it went farther along. Crawling on their bellies they came to a place where they could easily stand up and breathe a little air through a crack (which saved their lives).

The next morning, Sunday, at roll call, we felt the slave drivers' bad mood, which came out during the convicts' washing and bathing when they constantly insulted us. They gave more than a dozen of us two nights in prison and two days of dry bread, which they could do without going through the committee.

Around eight o'clock Corbin came to the crib and asked me if there was anything new.

"No, the Captain of Arms, like on every Sunday, made me march over here and I was surprised not to see you. I guess you were out hunting David and Ballin? They're good guys, you know them, it's only natural that they would try to be free and it's not up to you, sentenced like them, to prevent them. It's the guards' business and not the convicts'."

"You're right, Duval. I know them both. They were in my convoy and I respect them because they're not loudmouths like so many others who are all talk but never do anything. And if they try to hurt them, I'll stop it."

Those were the words that this wretch used. And he left and came back a half hour later along with the convict Bonacorsi whom he had got as a volunteer for a chore. This guy came with him because he was bored in his cabin and wanted to get some fresh air for a minute. Corbin asked me to fill up his empty canister halfway with gasoline. I had no idea what it was for. When I asked him he answered: "We're going to do some cleaning."

I figured it was to destroy some insects or ticks or something like that at a guard's house.

An hour later I found out from Bonacorsi, when he came back fuming with anger and rage to his cabin, that Corbin had taken another man for the chore, got some old blankets from the storeroom, doused them in gasoline, put them in the excavation where David and Ballin were no doubt hiding and set the thing on fire to smoke them out.

They did not suffocate, thanks to the crack they had found. I really want to believe that it was done on the orders of the new boss guard and the guard of the first class acting as Captain of Arms and not on the order of Commandant Leboucher. Which does not take the responsibility off the head of the warden, the little omnipotent king.

But he had to accept the second ignominy the following day when they brought miners from Saint Joseph promising them bonuses without telling them what it was for so that they would not refuse like the miners of Royal Island probably would have done. (They were wrong. I knew those employed to blow up the rocks and if they knew it had to do with blowing up David and Ballin, they would not have refused. This might astonish the reader, but it's true.)

A team of four miners came from Saint Joseph, one of whom was Rozier, a little guy from my convoy who, though treated with caution, almost always had work, always tried to cozy up to both sides and was hoping for a pardon, which his relatives were working on. He was outraged when he learned about the work that they were going to make him perform. He expressed his fury to me and did the same when he got back to Saint Joseph. Simon and all the comrades couldn't believe him.

After the explosion they were surprised at not finding the mashed up bodies of David and Ballin. The dynamiters did not understand.

"Yet they really were hiding there and didn't run away. They were well guarded," they said. "How can we not find them choked by the smoke or blown up by the dynamite? It's too much, it's like magic …"

Here's what happened. After having escaped from choking thanks to the crack, seeing their hunters' dirty tricks, they thought that maybe their executioners would be capable of dynamiting them. They decided to leave at any cost since bullets were still less frightening than an explosion.

The night was dark and they snuck out without arousing the attention of their half-asleep guards on watch. They went down to the dock to look for a board or something that could help them land on the continent where, if they had a chance of escaping notice, they would have a good chance of being able to get a dinghy since they wouldn't be suspected of being escapees because they would still be watched over in their hiding place.

The poor men found nothing but two big bags of hoe and pickaxe handles that had not been returned to the storeroom. They each took one and got on top, but the water knocked them off. With nothing to hang onto, they had to give up this last hope, not to say these scraps of wood that had been of no help to them since most of them did not even float. And these handles finally betrayed them when they were fished out on the dock the morning after the explosion.

An official hunt throughout the island began again without finding anything. It was the Sergeant Major's dog that barked and gave away their new hiding place. They happened to hide in an officer's cabin, once used by Commandant Leloup, near the barracks that was under repair. In the vast interior there was another cabin, inhabited by the Major. The latter, drawn by the barking of his dog that refused to answer his calls, wanted to find out what was going on and he found the two fugitives, who told him who they were and asked for his protection so that they wouldn't be murdered by the guards raging after them. He told them that he could not be made their accomplice and he was going to inform the Internal Service, but that they would not be mistreated.

As soon as they were informed, the boss guard with the bulldog face and the Captain of Arms burst into the cabin and fired a shot without hitting anyone (however, in writing these lines I think I recall that Ballin was nicked). The Major told them off as they deserved, telling them that to act like that was to murder men who were exhausted and defenseless and he would not allow it, not wanting his dog, who had discovered them, to be the cause of a murder.

"Take them away and do it without hurting them in any way, otherwise I'll report it. Come on," he said to David and Ballin, "don't be scared and I'll see you in the cell."

Seething with rage the two murderers took them away, cursing the Major who prevented them from earning their respective ranks of principal guard and boss guard.

When they passed by to go to their prison, I left my work and went as close to them as possible, which made the Captain yell at me, "You want to get out of here. Get to work!"

I did nothing of the sort and exchanged a look of understanding with David and Ballin that under such circumstances had much to say: from me, my respect for their courage and my regret at being powerless to help them in their misfortune; from them, the satisfaction of being respected, understood and helped if possible. They were dirty, in rags, gaunt and haggard, with no sleep for three days and worn out by their emotions. I think that they had had some provisions prepared.

The Major kept his word, saw them in the cell and gave them what he could: a little milk. They were brought before the special court that granted a few extra years to their sentences. In the prison in Cayenne they tried to escape, but did not succeed. They returned to the Islands where they were put in the special area to serve out their prison sentences. These special area cells were graves. Most of the men who were put in them found their death there. When David and Ballin left, they were dying. They recuperated a short time in the hospital and in the camp and then were sent to the Incorrigibles in Camp Charvein [on the Maroni river]. They escaped. Ballin died, I don't know how. David succeeded in two ways: the good man was able to get a little money and went to Georgetown to look for his comrades who, since they could not get out of there, would probably have been recaptured.

I was surprised that Courtois had not been informed of this event, as well as Eugène Degrave, who didn't write about it in his book *Le Bagne*. Nevertheless, I think that it is an event worthy of mention and that the convicts on Royal Island at the time were not bound to forget it. And unless they had a short memory and nothing in place of a heart they were all disturbed by the atrocity and savagery of such acts against these two good and courageous comrades in Gehenna, David and Ballin.

❖ ❖ ❖

After this I went three days without seeing Corbin. When I saw him, I told him what I thought about what he did and asked him to find somebody else to take care of his tools because I did not want to see his face anymore—it made me sick because I found it so repulsive to act like that toward two poor men whom he said he respected. What would he have done if he hated them?

He tried to apologize, but I did not want to hear it and told him that everyone who had a little heart left in him would spit in his face for trying to suffocate David and Ballin, two escapees who maybe would have been acquitted. He understood that I was speaking the truth and asked to be made a foreman in the prison where he became assistant executioner of the hatchet man Chaumet.

He was replaced by the guy who had taken my place in the works. After he accepted being a foreman, he became a first-class ass, in charge of watching me.

During this time Girier went to Saint Joseph Island in October 1893 a few days before the capture of David and Ballin. Like me he was sorry about our separation, but he found a small group of comrades who all ate together and talked together. On November 11 (strange coincidence that it's on this very day that I am writing these lines), the anniversary of the execution of our comrades in Chicago [the Haymarket Martyrs in 1887], I received a note from him telling me that all the comrades scattered in different cabins would get together that evening to hear a talk in memory of the late comrades. He was sorry that Pini and I could not be among them.

He worked as a gardener and was happy to grow things. He put a lot of work into it and tried out different things. He asked Simon to work with him, but I don't know if the camp boss allowed it.

On Royal Island the first class Major named Pierre arrived. After learning that Pini, an anarchist, was in his service, he kicked him out the minute he began to feel a little better.

So 1893 ended …

❖ ❖ ❖

At the very beginning of January I was promoted to second class. This annoyed me a lot because I was going to change cabins, be separated from

Pini and find myself alone. Deliberately or not, I do not know, they forgot to make me leave the stone cabin. I was very careful not to say a word. Pini no longer slept in the prison after he got out of the hospital, nor did Girier since his arrival on Saint Joseph. It was only later that Pini went back again into the hospital and since it was absolutely necessary for what we wanted to do I asked the guard Raymond why they left me in the stone cabin. He told me that I should have said something earlier, that they had forgotten, but the mistake would be corrected right away. Indeed, that very night I slept in the cabin with the men of my class, across from the pharmacy and the military hospital.

Before leaving the cabin I have to say what happened a few days after my nomination to second class: Buenerd's escape attempt.

He was supposed to leave with one of his comrades who had been able to get some materials from his work to build a raft to reach the continent. It was difficult to leave the stone cabin, watched as it was. You had to saw through a bar or bend it. For this Buenerd had got a big cord. He asked me to do him a favor and bring some hay from the cowshed to make a dummy so the rounds wouldn't notice he was gone. Even though it was dangerous, I did not want to refuse the poor man his means of escape. On the day agreed I brought enough grass and hay for us to make the dummy after the first round.

He went to the window in the cabin's toilet and forced open the bar. The minute he stuck his head through, three shots were fired by the guard on duty. Buenerd was not hit and right away we tore apart the dummy and threw the grass in the stalls. Everyone in the cabin saw us (it was a useless precaution since it was found in the defecation tubs). We had not even finished when all the slave drivers burst into the cabin and made everyone get up and strip down completely naked. Then there was a general inspection that lasted two hours. I'm not exaggerating when I say that the guard who inspected me took no less than twenty minutes, hoping to find some little scratch to establish my guilt. He went away empty-handed. (But, oh, how humiliating it all was.)

Buenerd alone was put in the cell. They knew all about his attempt. He had been denounced, but by whom? We never knew.

The next day I was summoned to the Internal Service. The boss guard and the guard Raymond told me about the whole thing in detail, how it had gone down, how I had brought the grass, etc. They told me this with a friendliness that I didn't think they were capable of.

Raymond said to me, "Admit it, Duval, you see that we know everything. It's no use denying it. I promise you that there will be no consequences for you. We don't want any harm to come to you, only good. Proof is that you've been promoted to second class."

To admit it would have been to give myself up to their mercy. To deny it was repulsive to me.

I found a way out by saying to them, "Do you think, gentlemen, that I wanted to escape and I made these preparations with this end in view?"

"No, we know that it was Buenerd and we know who his accomplice is."

"Then what are you charging me with, seeing that it wasn't my escape attempt."

"Maybe not, but you helped them by bringing grass to make the dummy."

"That's not proven and who will prove it? Bring him here in front of us." (I knew that they were being very careful not to do this.)

"So you don't want to say anything?"

"Gentlemen, I have said it."

"To the cell and you'll pay dearly for it!"

I left and the boss guard yelled to the prison guard to put me in double irons.

All the men in the cabin were interrogated and all of them said that they had seen nothing, that they had been woken up by the shots fired. When Buenerd was interrogated he in turn denied that I had supplied the grass or helped him in any way. He also cleared his accomplice of whom they had no physical evidence since he'd had time in the morning to get rid of everything. Three hours after that I left the cell and only Buenerd was punished with sixty days in solitary.

# Chapter 9
# When You Speak to Me Like That

A convoy arrived carrying the comrades [Louis] Chenal, [Henri Pierre] Meyrueis, [Jean-Baptiste] Foret, and [Joseph André] Crespin.

❀ ❀ ❀

They disembarked on Royal Island around eight in the morning among a detachment of around thirty men and were brought to the cowshed by a guard and two foremen, one of whom was responsible for watching me. The guard went to the Internal Service, so they remained under the watch of the two asses.

At the cowshed the fire was lit and I was preparing bread soup for Pini who could not build a fire in his garden. After looking at all these poor men, before asking if there was anything I could do, I set my sights on one of them who was calling out loudly for a cigarette. After giving him tobacco and paper I asked him if there were any anarchists in the convoy.

"Well, yes," he said to me in a heavy Parisian accent (he lived in Montmartre and was a house painter by trade).

He pointed out Foret and Meyrueis. I knew nothing of the sentencing of the latter. I found out later that he had been sentenced to life, along with another comrade sent to New Caledonia, for killing a snitch called "Le Petit Pâtissier" (The Little Dough Man). I knew from the newspapers that Foret had been sentenced to death and that Séverine [the famous female journalist] had taken a great interest in him.

So, I went to them with my hand held out. I could not have been more surprised at the cold welcome they gave me. It was even worse when I told them my name. They turned down my offers that I always made to comrades under such circumstances and they did not listen to the information that I tried to give them. This really upset me because I felt that they did not trust me. They ventured to ask news about Pini. I told them that he was working in the garden of the Internal Service and it was not easy for him to get away.

"Nevertheless, since the arrival of the convoy is keeping the service busy with work, I can send my foreman to go get him and you can shake his hand."

"Don't bother," they said to me.

I went back to work and did not bother with them anymore. At ten o'clock I returned to the cabin, brought the bread soup that I had offered them and while eating with Pini I told him about their cold welcome. He told me that since they had acted like that, it was good I didn't send for him.

During the siesta they did not leave them in the cowshed but brought them all into the prison courtyard. At the time there was a convict serving thirty days in the cell who was put to the chore of going to get the food provisions and distributing them to the punished men. Meyrueis and Foret talked with him and asked him if he knew me and if it was really me they had seen at the cowshed. They were surprised when he said yes, but even more so when he told them that he really thought I was a snitch.

At 1:00 p.m. they brought them all before the Internal Service. Around 1:30, Cayro, the orderly for the Internal Service, came to find me to tell me that there was an anarchist who wanted to see me before leaving for Saint Joseph.

"They're all leaving for Saint Joseph?

"Yes," he told me.

"What's the name of the guy who wants to see me?"

"Crespin."

I went to shake Crespin's hand. Foret and Meyrueis moved away and I returned with a heavy heart.

When they arrived on Saint Joseph, Foret right away said to Simon, the first one he saw, "I wasn't expecting to be so disappointed. I would never have believed that comrades in the penal colony would become snitches in order to have the right to make bread soup and have a freer hand than the other convicts."

When he explained what he was talking about, Simon said to him, "You say that again and I'll wring your neck!"

Then he told this to all the comrades, Girier, Faugoux, etc., who gave Foret such a reception that he did not dare say anything more. And they urged him to earn some respect like everyone else had done up until then. "If there are any comrades who seem to have a freer hand, even though they're watched more closely, it's because they were able to earn respect by their decent behavior, which gave them the strength to stand out. Do the same."

Foret and Meyrueis were taken aback, but nevertheless had been told that I was a snitch. That's how one is slandered and sullied by lying individuals. The chore man in the prison who had told them this had worked maybe a month at the cowshed leading two oxen with the barrel of water that they got from the sea to clean the hospitals, pharmacy, convent, and bureaucrats' housing when they needed it. When he was violent with the oxen, two good animals, Duplâtre, the cowherd, warned him several times not to mistreat them or else he would have him replaced. He paid no attention to him, so Duplâtre asked for another man to lead the oxen.

Being better off there than at the chores, he missed the work and wanted Duplâtre to have him sent back. One day when he was complaining to me, who knew what had happened, I disagreed with him and sided with Duplâtre. That was all it took to make me an enemy of this idiot who would not say aloud but suggested that I could be a snitch. If he had said this to a veteran, he would have been slapped, but with newcomers it worked out well, especially since the seed had been sown: Foret and Meyrueis were urged to be distrustful in this environment. I found this out when they came back to Royal Island. It was too late because the rat had left the Islands, otherwise he would have got what was coming to him. Foret and Meyrueis apologized, sorry for having put any trust in the words of a vile slanderer.

I saw Lepiez and Paridaën for the first time when they came to the hospital. I had good conversations with them and was able to appreciate these two good comrades. Paridaën had quickly recovered from the onset of dysentery. It did not go so well for Lepiez who did not have the necessary treatment and because he was sensitive, was never able to recover and stayed sick all the time. This caused a lot of problems with the slave drivers. Under all circumstances he was very dignified and able to gain respect for his ideas.

During his stay in the hospital I saw him often. Paridaën told me he was an individualist, so I had a few, very polite discussions with Lepiez about this new theory that I was unaware of. It did not take me long to see that it was a useless label. For, like us anarchist communists, he wanted the most complete freedom for individuals and their right to the full satisfaction of their needs. The maximum of well-being for the minimum of effort. That's what the anarchist communists fight for. And what do the individualists fight for? Isn't it for the same thing? So what good are all these labels that sow confusion and discord among the best comrades, the militants?

When he left the hospital Paridaën stayed on Royal Island, which allowed me to appreciate his upright, generous nature. Having been punished in the cell for maintaining his dignity toward an ignorant slave driver, he did not hesitate to sacrifice himself to make it easier for two comrades in the cell to leave and attempt an escape that they had already prepared ...

❊   ❊   ❊

Pini had to have another medical exam and was admitted to the hospital by the Sergeant Major. The following morning the Major of the first class,

Pierre, who had already discharged him because he was an anarchist, seeing him in his service again said to the nun, "Sister, our profession is painful sometimes, being forced to treat individuals whom we find unacceptable."

Sister Antoinette, to whom he said this, not being an idiot, answered him in such a way that made him remember the noble profession he practiced (which he was unworthy of). He kept Pini in his service and took care of him.

To show how his junior colleague was as well: a few days after Pini entered the hospital, I went to the medical visit that was being held in the prison courtyard because of some repairs to the roof of the infirmary. I appeared before the Major to have him sign a voucher to make a pair of shoes with cloth uppers, since I had the right to a pair of shoes every six months and I had been wearing mine for seven. I was careful with them because I always had trouble getting a new pair. I showed him my feet, which were deformed by rheumatism. He sent me away without saying a word and as I was leaving I heard him say to the two guards who were present, one from the prison and the other accompanying the sick, "Look at him. He deformed his own feet to get out of being a soldier."

The prison guard, who had been on Royal Island for a few years and knew the trouble I had getting shoes every time, said nothing in response, but seemed not to agree with the Major.

The Major saw this and said to him, "You don't believe me. Watch, I'm going to make him admit he's faking."

I heard all this and just shrugged my shoulders, but it was different when the so-called man of science, that imbecile, called me by my name, informally using "*tu*," and then "Come here, you!" to which I did not answer. He was floored. The prison guard was not at all surprised because he understood why I did not respond to his call. So he called me [using the polite "*vous*"], "Well, come on, Duval, the Major's calling you."

"When you speak to me like that, I answer."

And I appeared before the Major, shaking with anger. If the two guards were not there, I would have jumped on him and strangled him. While looking at him straight in the face, in the eyes (which he lowered), I heard him ask, "How'd your feet get deformed?"

"Rheumatism contracted during the War of 1870. As you see, I did not deform my feet to get out of being a soldier, but the opposite. It's because I was a soldier that my feet are ruined and not without horrible pain, as you must be aware of, Major Sir ..."

After this answer he did not know what to say to me and told Allmayer to make the voucher for the shoes right away so that he could sign it. Never had I seen a man so shamefaced and irked that this had to happen in front of the convicts and two guards. I do not know if the prison guard had little sympathy for this Major or it was simply because he was his superior, but he seemed delighted by the disappointment—I understood this by his look, with a shadow of a smile.

Lepiez left the hospital, returned to Saint Joseph and worked on the butte dragging the wheelbarrow, which was too much for him and they knew it, but seeing that he asked for nothing, they left him to it. Too proud to complain to his executioners, he kept at it until he dropped, went back to the hospital for three weeks and returned to Saint Joseph almost as sick as when he entered the hospital. They gave him a little easier work and it went on like that.

Pini also left the hospital a little bit better, but the camp diet brought him down right away. Every day I made him soup with the few little things we could get and he was able to manage. I think he must have been dying to return to the service of Major Pierre. In the garden of the Internal Service he was relatively calm. And since he had organized it tastefully, they were satisfied with him. Just like me, they were content to watch him but not bother him.

Until the day when there came from Cayenne a guard of the first class also named Pierre who replaced the marching boss. The second day of his arrival he began hassling us in the morning march to work. When he saw me alone he asked what construction site I belonged to. They told him my name and employment. At the one o'clock resumption of work he made me march without saying a word, looking at me straight in the eyes. I did the same without lowering mine. The next morning when my turn to march to work came he said to me, "Hey you, get going, famous man."

I was going to ask him the reason for this name, but I did not have time. At the one o'clock march, it was different when he said it again. I asked him why. Not knowing what to say he became arrogant and rude. I recalled him to politeness in a way that everyone understood. Right away the boss guard (the one with the face of a bulldog) ordered me put in chains in solitary. An hour later he came to see me and asked why I had spoken like that to the Captain of Arms. I pointed out that I had never used that language with his predecessor because he had always been decent to me, which for my part forced me to be so with him. But if someone provokes me, I answer like I have to. There is a gulf between guards and convicts. Each should stay on his side.

"That's what you have to make your subordinate understand, the guard in charge of the march who shouldn't call me by such names when I'm leaving for work. Twice today he called me 'famous man' and he said it ironically. What did he mean?"

"I didn't know about that, but you know, we're not afraid of you here."

"Me neither. I'm afraid of no one and if you attack me, I'll defend myself and immediately the sheep turns into a lion."

"But we're not attacking you, we mean you no harm."

"So why am I in the cell? Is it because I didn't want to let myself be ridiculed by a guard who just arrived in this penitentiary? I think that I'm the one who's right and that it's the guard whom you should berate so that such a thing not happen again, instead of putting me in the cell where I can stay as long as you like since not only are the regulations that we suffer more or less arbitrary, but the system is completely at your will."

"You know, Duval, if I report you for what you've just said to me, you'll be punished with ninety days in the cell and even the hole in the special quarter?"

"As you like. Up to this day I have always said what I think under any condition. That's my right and they've never punished me, obviously because the evidence proved me right. Today the case is the same. That's why I don't mind using such language with you."

"Okay, get out and don't pay attention to such trifles."

"Trifles for you maybe, but not for me."

No doubt the guard Pierre got orders not to amuse himself like that anymore because he didn't do it again. He just gave me a hateful look at every march. He really wanted to catch me doing something wrong so he could make a report and get his revenge. That's why he passed by so often. He did the same to Pini, but he always found us at our work, so he had no hold over us.

One day when he came by a little later than usual, he saw the furnace lit and a mess kit inside. When he asked about it I answered that I was making bread soup.

"You don't have the right! Get rid of that mess kit."

"Well, no. The bread and the lard that I make the soup with are mine and I won't throw it away."

"Throw it away or I'll do it for you."

"Do it, if you dare."

And saying this I stood close to him and if he had made one move to throw away my bread soup, I would not be writing these lines because I would have poured it over his head and then split his head open with one of the machetes I was organizing. He didn't try it. He just stroked the butt of his gun—It was lucky for him that he didn't take it out. Going away he said to me that I wouldn't be bringing the bread soup back to the cabin.

"Good luck to whoever's going to stop me because for that he'll have to kill me. What's it to you if I eat my ration of bread and lard cooked together? It does no harm to the administration. Your predecessors understood that and never said anything to me. It's simply your viciousness. And why? What did I ever do to you?"

"I'm telling you that you won't bring that bread soup back and I'm going to make a report that you insulted me."

"Make two if you want, I'll be able to say what happened and that it's a lie that I insulted you. The provocation came from you, not me."

"Be quiet, goddamnit, or I'll bring you to the cell right away."

"Not before going by the Internal Service where there will be an explanation. I'm not going to put up with your tantrums."

He went away seething with anger and rage. At 5:00 p.m., after all the tools had been put back, I brought the bread soup back and gave it to the watch of the stone cabin to hand over to Pini. No one was there to stop me. The next morning I was summoned to the Internal Service to answer to what had happened with the Captain of Arms. After explaining everything, I was authorized to make bread soup whenever I wanted, since it didn't get in the way of my work. The guard Pierre must have keeled over in anger.

I think the guard Raymond, who was employed in the Internal Service and whom I did not find unlikable, must have been mixed up in the matter. Otherwise, brutes like that would have certainly made some ludicrous reports about me that would have tasted very sweet to the new Commandant Deniel, who had just replaced Leboucher.

Foret had asked this new little kinglet to work as a baker, which was his profession. He accepted with no problems. It was different for Chenal who asked to practice his trade as a carpenter. They asked him a bunch of questions and made him wait fifteen days before sending him off to the works.

In my new cabin I had an argument with an imbecile that would have degenerated into a brawl without the intervention of Georges and De Labusta. He tried to insult Pini because on a few Sundays, when he was in the hospital, Pini went to mass and to vespers (which left a very bad impression on the camp). Knowing why and not being able to tell, I was very embarrassed to have to answer when someone said to me, "It's not the place for an anarchist."

I said, "He's bored at the hospital and loves music and singing. That's why he spends some time there."

Whoever was not happy with that answer I put in their place, asking them what right they had to tell him what to do when he did them no harm, etc. See, Pini was going to the church to see a convict who acted as an intermediary to the chaplain from whom he wanted to get a little money. I tried to talk him out of it, but he wouldn't listen to me and we almost got into a fight. When he failed (which I foresaw) he was sorry and agreed with me, cursing the guy who had given him this tip as certain. Later Meyrueis wanted to try to get money the same way; I was able to talk him out of it by citing the case of our comrade Pini.

During this time Émile Henry was getting them to talk about dynamite in Paris. And a bragging idiot got himself interviewed by the journalists while pretending to be Pini, on whose head the attacks came down. The whole press talked about Pini so much that the administration was alarmed and the Governor of Guiana came to the Islands to make sure that Pini was really there and not in France. It was a guy named Placeau in 1898 who told me that it was [Léon] Ortiz who played this game pretending to be Pini. I don't know if this is true or not.

❊   ❊   ❊

Faugoux was still sick and came back to the infirmary on Royal Island. A few days later it was Chevenet's turn to return to the hospital and he told me that Plista was probably going to come a little later and I could see and talk with him. He let me in on the problems between him and Girier.

I forgot to talk about a comrade named [Auguste] Hincelin who was always very dignified before his slave drivers. I think he came on the convoy before Foret, Meyrueis, and Chenal. Before Girier got thrown in the prison, all three of us had some good conversations. He was intelligent and had a very good understanding of the libertarian ideas that he had started to learn from [Auguste] Liard-Courtois, his first teacher. He often spoke to us about him and in terms that made me want to meet this comrade and shake his hand in friendship. I had no idea at the moment that this desire would be realized so soon, and in this hell.

Hincelin was sent to Saint Joseph with the other comrades. I have always held him in high esteem, despite his quirks.

❊   ❊   ❊

Crespin did not associate with the comrades on Saint Joseph (besides, I don't know if he was really a comrade). He was sent back to Royal Island where he tried to escape on a raft. He failed, was given sixty days in the cell and sent to Cayenne.

Before continuing I should go back in order to correct an oversight a short time before Commandant Leloup left the Islands. And it's comrade Simon that I am thinking about.

While Lévy and Allmayer were in the cell after being unmasked in that heinous plot against us, Commandant Leloup wanted information, so he interrogated the comrades who were scattered on the two islands. That was how one morning, being with Girier in front of the Internal Service, I saw little Simon for the first time. But it wasn't possible to speak with him. He was on the other side with a guard next to him. We waved to each other in friendship. During this time the two daughters of the Commandant passed in front of us, one was around seven years old and the other nine. Beautiful children with curly blonde hair, but proud and arrogant like their mother, and oh, how they looked at the convicts with contempt and scorn! But because they had seen their father talking with me at the accountant's, whose little boy was so happy to play with and hug the "lock-mit," as he said … (These details to show the good nature of this late comrade) … a minute of the guard's absence was enough for Simon to come throw himself in our arms. Ah! How happy the three of us were in this brief instant.

And during this moment Simon said to us, "What beautiful children just went by. How nice it would be to like them, but all we can do is hate them because with their faulty upbringing, which will only become worse in such an environment, I feel like they hate us and scorn us and always want to hurt us, even though we want nothing but the best for them. Ah, what a society!"

These words touched us deeply. Girier and I embraced him. At this moment the guard responsible for watching him came back and threatened to report us. All three of us answered that he might just as well make four reports if he wanted, it would take nothing away from the unappreciable joy that we'd just felt in this brief instant.

The guard Raymond heard this, saw Simon getting all worked up, and asked what was going on. After our answer he told off his colleague saying to him that he should not have gone off like that, even though he knew very well that we were not supposed to communicate together, especially before the interrogation. Then he asked Girier and me where our guard was.

"We don't have one. A foreman came to get us at our work to come here and you're the one who said to wait here. See, we haven't budged."

"Okay, wait for the committee and afterward I will authorize you to talk."

The committee was composed of the Commandant, the works leader, the boss guard and the guard Raymond as clerk of the court. I was called first.

The first question the Commandant asked me was, "Do you know an anarchist named Rousseau?"

"Yes, he's a very well known militant. He came to see me in La Santé Prison before I left for Avignon."

"It seems he's very rich."

I couldn't help smiling when I said to him that there were no anarchist brothers who were rich, otherwise we would be more successful. "Rousseau owns a little wine shop and somehow lives off that. He's a good comrade, very sincere and very well respected."

"You're not telling us the truth about his wealth because it's been proven that he chartered a boat to help the anarchists on the Islands to escape."

"Ha! Commandant, today you know very well that it's a lie, a despicable ploy of Allmayer. There's plenty of proof of that."

"Nevertheless," he said to me, smiling despite himself, "there are all the usual signs. Do you deny that, too?"

"They had to complicate matters to give it a semblance of truth, but let me tell you, Commandant, how surprised I am that you fell for it like that."

He asked me a few insignificant questions, then it was Girier's turn, whom he asked the same questions. His answers, from what he told me, were the same as mine.

❖ ❖ ❖

We returned right away to our work and didn't see Simon again. Later we found out that they hassled him over the question of the notes hidden in the rocks—maliciousness, seeing that Allmayer was caught red-handed by the boss guard on Saint Joseph and the mystery was uncovered.

The next day Bordier was interrogated, as well as the stonecutter, and the file would have been closed if Allmayer, on leaving the cell and returning to Royal Island, had not lodged a complaint with the Commission and asked that I be cited as a witness in order to prove that he had nothing to do with the escape planned by Herbette and Pierson and that, on the contrary, it was hatred of the convicts that drove him to foil this attempt in the interest of the administration.

He was obviously planning to redeem his disgrace like this and get a job (doing nothing). But he did not know that during his stay in the cell I had learned why the rat had made us miss such a great escape (his too), and it was going to come down on his head.

As soon as the Commission members were set up, they came to get me at work. Allmayer was already there and we both entered the Internal Service where this scene was destined to take place, which was unforgettable to me and to all those who were witnesses of it. For, if the boss guard and the guard Raymond had not pulled Allmayer out of my hands, I would have strangled him. I had to be satisfied with slapping him and spitting in his face.

He began like this: "Sirs, I lodged this complaint and cited the deportee Duval, who was the heart of Pierson's and Herbette's escape. I appeal to you in good faith and you can judge it by the sincerity of his anarchist convictions, which I condemn along with most of those who profess these ideas, but who are only crooks and dogs."

It was then that I jumped on him and they snatched him out of my hands (what strength they find at such times because it took a lot of strength for them to manage this). So, I could only slap him and spit on him full in the face while saying to him, "Rat! Anarchists have a moral courage that you don't, since you cited one as witness. And not one person present here who knows you would do you the same honor, since they also know what a sordid creature you are, a disgrace to humanity."

The Commandant urged me to calm down so that Allmayer could continue. It was then that he cited himself as having foiled the escape in the interest of the administration.

"And Duval can tell you if I'm telling the truth."

"Rat! As always, you lie!"

And I told the story as I knew it. Allmayer, did not know that I was so well informed and was dumbstruck and did not know what to say. The Commandant sent him away like a dog and made me stay there to congratulate me on having cleared up the matter.

"Commandant, I don't deserve it. It's due to a chance circumstance that I can't tell you about."

"Like always, your reticence. But now are you going to deny this escape attempt?"

"No, Commandant, today I admit it."

"And will you do it again?"

"Yes, Commandant, as long as I have the strength and energy to get back what they took away from me—my freedom."

"And for this you'll take away my lifeboat?"

"Yes, Commandant. I'm only waiting for the opportunity."

"Yes, but I'm here and I'm watching. It's your sincerity that is stopping me from putting you in the cell for daring to answer me like that and having to put up with such a scandal in front of the Commission."

"Commandant, don't I have the right to be outraged at seeing myself insulted along with my friends in what is so precious to us, I mean our convictions?"

"Which, fortunately, we are far from seeing realized."

"Of course, but we've had the satisfaction of fighting for them, of following our predecessors and always moving toward the best."

He dismissed me.

# Chapter 10
# The Anarchist Plate

A chore group of fifteen men came from Saint Joseph to quarry some stones to use for making filters for the gentlemen guards and all the personnel. They also took the opportunity to make some for the friends of the other penitentiaries and forest worksites. They did not watch them so closely or bother the convicts' labor when it was to their benefit. For a pack of tobacco, which cost them only three sous, they had a filter well made by a stonecutter.

Simon was part of this chore, which a guard I knew was with and who was devoted to his duty but not mean. There was also an Arab foreman with them who was not too nasty. I knew him well. He had been in the same cabin with me on Royal Island. I was surprised to see him as a foreman when he came with the men to get shovels and picks and I could not help asking him, "You're a pig now?"

"No, I'm not mean, I don't hurt the men."

A voice rose up to agree with what he said, "We could only wish that all the pigs on the Islands were like him."

What a nice surprise to recognize Simon voicing these words! What a good, friendly handshake we gave each other! Then I slipped to him, "Break the handle of your pick. You'll come back to get another and we can talk."

The worksite to quarry the stones was behind the cowshed so it was easy. An hour later Simon came with the foreman to get a new pick handle. I brought him into the tool crib and embraced the young comrade, whom I loved like a son and was happy to be with. He felt the same.

Before he went back to the worksite, I said to the Arab, "At ten o'clock the guard's going to eat at the mess and you'll be guarding the men during the siesta. I'm going to tell Gosset to warn the Internal Service that I won't be returning to the cabin and you'll let Simon come eat with me. You have nothing to fear, neither from me nor him, we won't cause you any problems."

"I know and you can count on me, even if the guard hangs around and gets his food brought to the worksite."

Through Gosset I got a liter of wine and a box of sardines for the feast—the good fortune of spending two and a half hours with a comrade, which would have been so much better if Girier and Pini could have been with us.

At 10:15 Simon was next to me. At 12:30 he went back to the worksite. Since these two hours were short, we had a lot of things to say to each other and a lot to ask. We talked long about comrade [Auguste] Viard, whom I had known, as well as other comrades. He made me familiar with Ravachol and made me appreciate him even more.

On his way to meet me, Simon found a pouch on the road that was almost full with tobacco, cigarette papers, and six sous. Right away he gave me this pouch, telling me to look for the owner and give it back to him because it could only belong to a poor man like us. It was a little thing, but very often it is in the little things that we can best judge a man for the big things. Such was the case for this late comrade Simon, whose courage, energy, kindness, and loyalty stood out to the end.

A little later I made the acquaintance of Thiervoz, who, despite his sturdy physique and his Herculean strength, fell sick and was admitted to the hospital on Royal Island. His complacency (not through baseness, but because he had to use his strength in the work) got him appreciated by the ward's Sister, who, when he was almost cured, asked for him as a nurse. It was granted. Then I saw Thiervoz every day and we talked about Simon, whom he loved like a son and kept under his protection. Simon did not need that because he was capable of commanding respect on his own.

Nevertheless, against these disgusting individuals like you meet in the penal colony (I won't trace back to the cause), force is often required.

That's how one day Thiervoz gave a thrashing to one of these sorry individuals who was constantly hanging around Simon and often giving him a ration of bread and tobacco. Simon thought he was a generous man and sensitive to the sufferings of others whom he helped as much as he could. Also, understanding nothing about Thiervoz's intervention, he criticized him. But when the latter explained to him what the selfish aim of this so-called good heart was, Simon went with Thiervoz to find him and ask him for an explanation. He asked him to leave the cabin and go with him alone to show him that he needed no one else to command respect. The coward would not accept the invitation, so Simon had to be satisfied with spitting in his face and paying back his rations of bread and tobacco over the course of a month ...

❖   ❖   ❖

Commandant Deniel left the Salvation Islands and was replaced by Bonafai (the morphine addict). The boss guard and the Captain of Arms Pierre had just left the Islands. The former was replaced by a guy named Vannoni (nicknamed the Shepherd), a former sergeant major, a good accountant, but gutless and gifted with extraordinary stupidity. The second was replaced by a guard of the first class, a Corsican like himself, whose name I forget.

So, there were the little king and his lieutenant to whom we were going to be subjugated. On Saint Joseph the events that were about to unfold under these characters' administration would prove their barbarity and ferocity. Yes, barbarous, cruel, and ferocious, words too gentle to express their deceitfulness and savagery.

Straightaway Bonafai showed his hatred for anarchists and sided against them, telling Vannoni that he did not want any anarchist to have a job, even in the works, practicing his trade. Right away his lieutenant Vannoni was ready to obey all orders no matter what they were. He tried to take me out of the tool repair and abolish the job. The guard Raymond pointed out to him the usefulness of the job and that I did it conscientiously and he also pointed out the benefits that the administration got from the repairs, which were not done before.

"I don't care," the brute said. "The Commandant's order is that the anarchists should be in the chores and forced to do the hardest labor."

"That's not fair," Raymond hazarded, "and as far as Duval, you won't succeed. He's classed in the light work since he moved up from the works."

"I don't care," the brute said again, "he'll go to the chores like the others."

"Don't believe it," the guard Raymond told him. "The anarchists are more conscious of their dignity than the other convicts. They behave well and avoid punishment. On the other hand, they know how to assert their rights and if you act like this against them, you'll be forced to admit it, especially regarding Duval, Pini, and Girier, whom I know very well, better than the others."

This conversation between the chief, vicious idiot and his subordinate, who was more just and especially more intelligent than him, was reported by De Labusta, a secretary in the Internal Service after he left the hospital service, a job that Allmayer made him lose in order to better deceive Major Pierre. De Labusta heard everything and reported the conversation to me word for word, even with some commentaries by the guard Raymond on the matter. Thus warned, we were waiting every day for Commandant Bonafai's dirty trick. It didn't take long in coming. Pini was in the garden of the Internal Service and thus well placed to be watched closely and they also let Girier learn his lesson and be overworked in his job as gardener on Saint Joseph.

Mine no doubt bothered them and in order that the prejudice not be too obvious, here is how the smart Vannoni (called the Shepherd) found a way to take me out. A few days earlier a young guard named Renucci arrived from Cayenne, a compatriot of Vannoni and at least as stupid as him. He was chosen to catch me doing something wrong. As a result, whenever he was on duty in the camp, I constantly received visits from him at work, without him breathing a word to me.

Now, one evening, a little before bedtime, Georges and Dachet, who were both employed in the pharmacy, as soon as they got back to the squad, started singing a duet pretty quietly. De Labusta joined in at times. Since it was pretty nice to hear, I stayed close by, not breathing a word, just sitting on the bar they attach the hammocks to. All of a sudden the door opened and the guard Renucci and a foreman burst into the cabin. The song stopped immediately.

Renucci came up to me and said, "Your name and number."

"You know very well what my name is and as for my number, you can read it on my jacket."

He looked at me and said, "You're talking to me like that?"

"Yes, you ill-bred boy, what right do you have to address me informally, [with 'tu' instead of 'vous']?"

He saw his slip-up and said to me [using 'vous'], "Give me your name."

"Why?"

"You'll find out before the Commission."

"While I'm waiting, you can look for my name in the Internal Service."

After he left, Georges and Dachet apologized for singing, which was the reason why I was going to be punished.

"My friends, you have nothing to be sorry about, it was planned from the start. The silence wasn't broken. In the cabin of classed men no guard ever stopped us from talking and singing in a low voice like you were doing. The play is obvious. Why did this idiot come directly up to me and ask me for my name and number without finding out whether or not I was the one singing? You know, he isn't even smart enough to keep up appearances."

Then we talked about this with De Labusta who promised to keep me up to date about the scheme.

Two days later I went before the Commission and got thirty days in the cell. Vannoni wanted sixty, but the works leader saw by my answers that the report was stupid and vicious, so he opposed it.

They took me out for work to weed the north side of the prisons with a hoe. A guard was responsible for watching me and three or four sick men temporarily classed to light work. They were breaking rocks on the road. Among them was a guy named Paul Jacquemin, called Big Paul, a lifter like no other. He rummaged through the bags of his comrades in misery; everything was fair game to him. But a good heart who kept nothing for himself, the products of his pillage went to buy bread and tobacco for his comrades who were worse off than him, if they were in the cell. He respected me and was careful not to take anything at all from me. (I knew five or six sneak thieves like him who had no respect for others' petty things, but were basically helpful, discreet, good-hearted, and trustworthy men.)

One day when Renucci had been ordered to guard us on duty, he came up to me to watch me work, looking like he was scoffing at me. It took all my concentration, thinking about the escape plan on the arrival of the next convoy, not to split his head open with my hoe.

He went over to those breaking rocks and said to Jacquemin, "I'm not afraid of anarchists. They have to walk the line like everyone else. See, Duval insulted me and I made a report and I'll do it again at the first offense. I'm in charge of bringing him in line along with all the others."

I heard some of this, but was too far away to hear everything, which was reported to me by Paul Jacquemin, as well as the answer he gave, whose import I remember exactly: "I know Duval very well. Proof? Here's the poem I made up about him ..." And he recited it.

Renucci couldn't get over it and said to him, "You made that up?"

"Yes," Paul answered, "and I've made up many others."

Indeed, in his spare time when he was in the cell, what often happened was that he made up verses like the rhymester he was. Some of them were about certain guards or bureaucrats that, if he had recited them, would have floored Renucci and got him thrown in the cell right away.

Since then Paul was a scholar to Renucci and he listened to everything he told him. And Paul did not believe that I had insulted him, knowing that I was too mindful of being respected not to respect another. "Now don't be fooled by it, I'm not sure that because he put up with the punishment, which was probably undeserved, that he would be ready to put up with a second. He could very well have done to you what he did to Rossignol?"

"What did he do to the guard Rossignol?"

"Rossignol was not a guard but a police sergeant who tried to arrest Duval in the name of the law. Duval answered, 'In the name of freedom, I'll strike you down' and he stabbed him, but it was badly aimed, otherwise he would have killed him as he intended.'"

"You're sure about that?" Renucci asked, trembling.

"Absolutely," Jacquemin answered, who wanted to have fun with the fright and give him some more, so he started telling him some anarchist exploits that existed only in his imagination.

Renucci was so scared that right after that he found me he said, "You know, Duval, there's no reason to bear a grudge against me for my report. I had to do it."

"So," I said to him, "it was a set-up? I thought so. Let it go this time, but if you start in again it won't go down the same way, I'm warning you."

"Nothing to fear, Duval, besides I don't want to stay in the Islands and I'm going to ask to go to the forest worksite. I'd like it better than here."

Two months later he left for Kourou.

❧    ❧    ❧

June 26, 1884, my thirty-day punishment was almost finished and I was aching for it, starting to get bored with that mind-numbing work pulling weeds and for nothing: wherever it was done, they made me start over again. In the morning De Labusta passed by and said to me, "Duval, a fellow anarchist has sent President [Sadi] Carnot to meet his maker."

It was impossible to ask him any more about it. Commandant Bonafai had just suddenly popped up from behind a little mound of rubble that was being used to build new cells in line with the prisons. He asked De Labusta what he was doing there.

"I came to bring an order from the Internal Service to the cowherd." (That was true.)

"Why are you talking with this punished man? What did you say to him?"

"Nothing, Commandant, just hello."

"It's forbidden, you know that. You'll earn yourself a punishment from me."

He let him go. Then Bonafai called me over to ask what De Labusta said to me.

"Nothing, just hello."

"Work and don't talk to anyone, otherwise I'll give you sixty days in the cell."

I wanted to have news about what I'd just learned, so I had to realize my powerlessness to do anything worthwhile but accept this from the despot without saying a word. When he'd left, I thought about the act of justice of our comrade and how happy I was to see that despite all the persecutions, there remained fighters on the go, valiant pioneers who will bring about collective action through their individual action.

The following day, at the time when I was marching off with Jacquemin and three or four sick men, light workers, Vannoni made me go to another chore to pull weeds in the camp. I stayed there only one day. The next day they put me back behind the prisons by myself. I was very surprised when, the morning that my thirty days in the cell were over, the guard responsible for the service of the disciplinary premises told me that I still had fifteen days in the cell to do.

"How's that? I only had thirty days."

"And another fifteen from the boss guard for talking with a convict during work."

I knew right away where that came from. There was no use protesting, it would result in only one thing—to make matters worse and that was the moment when I needed to be in the camp.

After I had done these new fifteen days in the cell, they put me in the stone cabin. I thought I'd been put back into third class, but they said nothing to me. I was careful not to ask about it, knowing that this was going to be the cabin where they would put the comrades who were going to arrive on the next convoy that we were expecting any day. I was glad to be there to shake their hands, as long as they did not send them straight to Saint Joseph Island.

They disembarked on Royal Island and were all put in the stone cabin. There were five of them: [Léon Jules] Léauthier, [Edmond] Marpaux, [Gustave] Marchand, [Placide] Catineau, and [François] Briens. Along with Pini, Meyrueis, Chenal, and me, there were nine of us in all. Foret had done time in the cell with me and I do not remember why he was sent to Saint Joseph Island.

❊ ❊ ❊

We set up as best we could on the camp beds, but space was lacking; we could not all sit together. I was the best placed. I had near me Marchand, Briens, and Catineau. The last two were both carpenters and knew [Joseph] Tortelier very well. We spoke long about this comrade whom I highly respected, as well as about other good comrades I was eager to hear news about. For their part, they asked for information about this or that, if it was easy to escape, etc.

"But no, my friends, otherwise I along with plenty of others would not be here."

Then there was the refrain I had heard before and would hear again after them: "Ah! I'll never get used to a life like this, no way. I'll find a way to take off."

"That's great, my friends, we'll talk about that tomorrow. But above all, one piece of advice: think about it the most and talk about it the least."

All the slave drivers were bustling about the convoy, leaving us a little more leeway, which allowed us to talk, quietly of course, for part of the night. The other comrades did the same.

Part of the convoy stayed on Royal Island. They waited two days for the distribution of their clothes without going to work. As for me, they did not put me back at my job and since there was no one to replace me to repair the tools, they were in an even more defective condition. A little later there were no more tools to give to the men on chores.

Ha! Good taxpayers, if you knew what the prison administration was in Guiana, you would be sickened by such a mess, such a waste of everything, not counting the thefts of the eminent bureaucrats. I'll cite only one thing that was important because for one year the convicts did not get shoes or clothes, at least in the Islands and I think it was everywhere. The shirts were worn very seldom and only for inspections; in the Salvation Islands we were allowed to cut them into pants and jackets. A sixty- or ninety-day punishment in the cell was the rule for willful tearing of clothes belonging to the State. This again proves that the Laws and Regulations are always in favor of those who make them.

The name of the bureaucrat who made the convicts walk barefoot and without clothes was the righteous Inspector Mercier, who, when he was Commandant in Maroni, sold the leather and cloth to the Dutch in Albina on the other side of the river Maroni.

❖   ❖   ❖

They started me sweeping the camp in the morning, pulling weeds in the afternoon or on various chores under the supervision and surveillance of a black from Guadeloupe. He was so proud of having the C.M. on his arm and of ordering men around, especially whites, that he took himself for the Governor of Guiana. Just to look at him made you want to slap him. When he gave orders, it was worse. But I got the opportunity to pull him down from his authoritarianism with respect to me. Then all was fine until the day when he committed a new offense.

On the day after the arrival of the comrades, during the siesta, I was talking for a long time with Léauthier and was glad to observe that this puny, sickly young comrade had a keen mind, the spirit of justice, a great strength of will, and extraordinary energy. He was respected by all the comrades of his convoy and was so gentle that the convicts in the stone cabin right away took a liking to him. They would help him in the smallest thing.

Marpaux and Marchand were two strong fellows, good guys, dead set on leaving that hell. Marpaux was very outgoing and showed that he was brave. Marchand was colder, more thoughtful, more of an observer. He was a comrade whom I got to know later, who earned all my trust and respect.

Briens was a good guy, generous and very cheerful, taking his situation more philosophically, which is not to say that he accepted it. He was hoping to escape and for that he did not lack courage. He would have taken action with his comrades in any plan whatsoever, provided that there was hope of freedom.

Catineau was sallow and constantly grumbling. He seemed in the biggest hurry to act. It needed the intervention of all his new and old comrades to keep him from doing something stupid. In spite of this, he was sometimes cheerful and he knew the whole repertoire of revolutionary songs, which he sang well. So, every evening, when we were shut up in the cabin waiting for the silence, we made him sing new ones.

We put Chenal, who was still in the works, in charge of getting a large tin plate made by the tinsmith. We managed to bring it back to the cabin and we inscribed on it in big letters, "Anarchist Plate," off which we all ate bacon and stew (but not soup). We all got together in the back of the cabin on the east side and by the window there, facing the camp, the guard on duty and the others saw us all eating together and singing in the evening. They watched and heard, but did not dare say a thing.

One day, there was a nice windfall. We got a hold of the newspaper recounting the defense of Émile Henry, which was read aloud during the siesta. Everyone in the cabin listened, as well as two guards who were by the window (and it must have taken seed). We never knew what they thought about the matter, we only saw them waving their arms as they went away, like men in a heated discussion.

The new comrades split up into different chores, which gave us hope that they would stay on Royal Island.

One day Léauthier was alone at a chore with a brute of a guard whose name I forget. This coward, seeing Léauthier's fragile constitution, taunted him and threatened to report him for unwillingness to work. He criticized what he did and his anarchist convictions, saying that he was not scared of anarchists and he would show them who was boss. Léauthier felt his dignity offended, straightened up, and showed this wretch how shameful his behavior was. And like under all circumstances he knew how to make himself respected, as well as his ideas and the people he struggled for. Then moving up close to him in order to snatch his gun in case he wanted to use it, he looked him straight in the face and he said, "And believe me that for this it's not necessary to be six feet tall and the size of Hercules."

The coward no doubt understood that if he could physically get the better of this little body with a weak constitution, morally it was another story. He had a force, a will, an energy that scared him, because he calmed down right away and urged Léauthier to do the same. But that was not an easy thing to do. At ten o'clock on the return from work, he sat in the corner with tears of anger. We asked him what the problem was. He did not answer at first. It was the men in the cabin who informed us about what happened at his chore. Right away the comrades went up to him to calm him down. He asked everyone for a weapon to kill this guard who thought he could get away with insulting him. Meyrueis showed such concern for him that a mother would have envied it. And he managed to calm him down.

Since that was the day it was my turn to take care of the plate, I could not be there at the scene. When the distribution had finished, I went to find Léauthier and try for myself to make him understand that in the situation in which we found ourselves, being so few, the loss of one individual like him was of great consequence. He understood that, took my hand, pulled me toward him, and hugged me. In the afternoon he returned to the same chore.

The guard acted politely and never started up again when he had anarchists in his chores.

Commandant Bonafai continued his petty annoyances, taking Chenal out of the works, saying that the anarchists should be on the chores and used for the hardest labor. Girier managed to get Simon accepted to work with him in gardening and both of them worked too hard at it. Girier was passionate about growing things and was eager to prove to the administration that something good could come if they left the convicts to themselves—a liking for their work. But Bonafai had a different understanding. When he found out that Simon and Girier were working together, he ordered Simon to be taken out of the garden. It still surprises me that he did not take Girier out of there, too.

Simon lost hope. He got so tired out by such a miserable existence and outraged by the petty annoyances, viciousness, and provocations of Commandant Bonafai that he resolved to do away with the spineless torturer, the vile inquisitor. Unfortunately he could not keep his secret because of the need to confide in those whom we love and trust. He let Girier in on it. He certainly could not have made a better choice because none of us were worthier of respect and trust. Girier talked him out of it, showing him that he should not despair because he was so young. As Liard-Courtois said in his *Souvenirs du Bagne*, in the chapter "Le Complot," page 184, Girier saved the life of Commandant Bonafai, who a few months later was going to have him condemned to death for an action that he not only did not commit, but in which he did not even participate and even tried hard to stop.

# Chapter 11
# The Saint Joseph's Massacre

On Royal Island all of us were fed up with the provocations of Bonafai, Vannoni, and the rest and we were waiting impatiently for the day of relief.

I did not speak with Courtois for long enough to inform him exactly about what had been arranged with Pini, and then with the comrades on Saint Joseph whose separation prevented us from carrying it out so that it was postponed until the arrival of the next convoy, which reinforced us with five energetic comrades with the same intention as us. And the behavior of Bonafai and his cronies justified us even more and quickened our fervent desire for the day when we would be able to put the plan into action. I will not go into details, I cannot. This is simply to set the record straight, for the love of truth. I was involved in this affair and I played a major role, so I can speak with full knowledge, especially since I am (alas!) the only survivor, except for Foret who I think learned about it on Saint Joseph.

After spending a few days in the stone cabin with the comrades, I asked to go back to the cabin of the classed men because it was absolutely necessary. They noticed their mistake and right away granted my request.

Things were going along just fine with the help of three convicts (even though they're dead I won't name them). When everything was ready, we intended it to be a totally peaceful action, except against those who tried to keep us from carrying out our plan: to take control of the situation and then escape.

It was set for Sunday morning. Allmayer and Lévy never knew about it. Nor did Plista, except maybe later through the comrades on Saint Joseph who themselves did not know on what day it would happen. Even those who would have desperately wanted to take part in it were not included. Since they were of no use to us, we were careful to keep them in the dark so that no mistakes would be made.

We did the same with respect to a few nonanarchist comrades who were men of action and serious, whom I knew well and could count on. Although we knew we could trust them, we were afraid that one of them would let one of his comrades in on it, so we agreed to tell them nothing until it was time to act. But alas, in spite of all the precautions that we took so carefully, our enemies who steal from us, exploit us, strip us of everything, murder us, and crush us with all that hypocritical, lying force in the name of the law, when for the love of truth and justice we raise our heads and tell them, "We've had enough," and we fight, it is often the unexpected that gets in the way of success and brings down those whom such a cruel society forces to do evil in order to get to the good.

So, there is prison, the penal colony, and the scaffold that are waiting for those who have committed the crime of wanting a harmonic society where the happiness of all can be found in that of each one of us.

Also in the penal colony, despite leaving nothing at all to chance, despite all the confidence in oneself and one's comrades in suffering, all the courage, energy and boldness that one can deploy to escape from one's executioners, there also you have to count on the unexpected. And it is all too true that the littlest causes often produce the biggest effects. Such was the case in our affair.

When I left the cell and went back to the stone cabin, the cabin guard had just been removed and replaced by Paul Jacquemin. He was put in the chores. He was carefree and young and only had eight years of hard labor, so he could hope to be freed and afterward we would see, he used to say. He accepted his situation with an extraordinary philosophy, singing all the time (and not badly). He was punished several times for this but never changed.

Everything was ready. A few days separated us from the act that would decide our freedom or death, no in between.

On Thursday, a week before the day so eagerly expected, the guard on duty during the first round was a Corsican, famous for his pretension, viciousness, and petty annoyances. (His name escapes me, but in writing these lines I can see his face again: taken as a whole it wasn't bad and wouldn't make you believe it could hide so much treachery, such a hypocritical mask.) Young and single he flirted with his partners' wives and one day he was almost caught red-handed with one of these ladies whose husband was in the hospital. The boss guard who made the discovery promised the lady to say nothing. Nevertheless, things leaked out and reached the ear of Commandant Bonafai, who reprimanded him and appointed him to Kourou on the next detachment. The Don Juan, who had come to the Salvation Islands as a patient following a fever contracted in the construction sites around Cayenne, got scared of this. So, he outdid himself in zealousness in order to get back into the good graces of the Commandant to cancel his transfer. He became more and more troublesome and did not miss the opportunity that came up on that Thursday evening.

The previous cabin watchman mentioned above was still humming after the broken silence. The guard made the foreman open the door and asked who was singing. No one answered.

"You don't want to tell me who's singing, okay. The entire cabin will be on dry bread for ten days."

As the offender did not give his name in spite of the threat, no one wanted to snitch on him out in the open. Besides, there was no need. The guard knew who always sang like that. But the opportunity was too good to miss. Knowing Bonafai's hatred and prejudice against anarchists, he made a report against us to please the despot, saying that the singing came from the back of the cabin where we slept, all the while knowing that the singing came from the middle of the cabin, since the singer slept right across from the door.

Pini and Chenal were left out of the report. Léauthier, Meyrueis, Marpaux, Marchand, Briens, and Catineau went before the Commission on Saturday. All of them were very dignified before the tyrant who, knowing they had no means of defense, scorned and insulted them, demanding them to be snitches by denouncing the singer.

All of them answered him in their turn, "It's up to the guard to tell you, that's his job and he knows very well that we weren't the ones singing. His report is intentionally false."

Since Meyrueis, Léauthier, and Marpaux went further in their answers, bluntly giving the Commandant a piece of their mind, all three were given sixty days in the cell. Marchand, Briens, Catineau were given thirty days. The cells were full, so two stayed in the stone cabin in full irons day and night.

Therefore, our opportunity was missed or at least postponed for two months, which was doubtful. Pini and I thought that when the punishment was over the comrades would be sent to Saint Joseph. That's what happened. Ah! I cannot tell you how much we cursed that idiot who was singing, without, however, being able to say anything to him about it. And that vile creep of a guard who just wanted to make his boss happy with that report, which did him no good in spite of all his baseness and platitudes—he was shipped off to Kourou before the comrades finished their punishment.

Pini and I were depressed by this foreman, that constant misfortune. Pini fell sick again and had to spend a few days in the infirmary. I could no longer make bread soup for him because neither of us had a penny to buy anything to improve the ordinary fare, which I could still digest even though it was disgusting. While for Pini the food made his sickness worse.

If we were not encouraging each other, if we were not supported by the idea that was dear to us with the hope of always doing better, we would have jumped headlong on our persecutors. And measures once taken, decided to go all the way, we would certainly have done a fine job.

Ah! How unfortunate that we did not act like that, that we did not get that satisfaction of a justified revenge in answer to so many provocations and humiliations. An act of justice that would have spared the death of our young comrades who were cowardly murdered two months later. And the tortures, the slow death in hideous suffering of our dearly missed comrade Girier-Lorion. Freed a few years later he would have escaped his slave drivers and with that ease of eloquence that he possessed and the sincerity of his convictions he would have spread the good word everywhere he went. And even if he stayed in the colony, along with the other comrades freed after him, firstly Lepiez and then some others—these comrades, in one way or another, would have been useful for propaganda, for spreading libertarian ideas.

The other comrades had long sentences, life or fifteen or twenty years of hard labor, and could have tried again. Even though Pini and I would no longer be part of it, we would have been usefully replaced by the comrades from the convoy of January 1895, such as Meunier Théodule, sentenced to life for blowing up the novice snitch Véry who was banking on the fat payment from the arrest of Ravachol by his brother-in-law Lhérot's denunciation, who was unfortunately not in the restaurant or was not hurt by the explosion, which spoiled our joy when we learned the news. But then, we found some compensation when the perpetrator got away. Later, sorrow followed upon the joy when we heard about the conviction of our comrade.

Being able to do nothing about it, Girier was longing for the day to shake the hand of Meunier. But unfortunately, he was bound to be refused.

Other comrades coming with him would, maybe, have taken part in the act. I say maybe because having known them and thinking about them again while writing these lines, I have my doubts, considering the difference in their sentences. Nevertheless, with the partnership of a few other well-chosen comrades, they could have seen the matter through for the best and succeeded. And so they, too, leaving this hell while young, would have been able to spread the good word and been useful for propaganda.

All this is only hypothesis. It very well could have happened that they would not have succeeded at all, that just like us they would have been massacred all together or tortured like our comrade Girier-Lorion and died the same way. In the meantime, both of us gave in to our executioners through our cowardice by not responding to their provocations and not revolting as was our intention, but on the contrary paralyzing each other in the vain hope of doing better. Today I can contemplate things more objectively: Was it not the instinct of self-preservation, the hope of seeing our loved ones again that paralyzed this spontaneous movement that had been brewing for so long?

And all this in spite of ourselves, in spite of the ideal that we held so close to our hearts making us so mindful of our dignity, which, however, we must admit that in spite of all our efforts to preserve it, we constantly left behind a little piece of it by accepting such a miserable existence.

What was result of our hesitation at the time?

The death of all our comrades, some murdered, others worn out and eaten away by the climate, the hardships, physical and moral suffering, and the lack of care in their sickness. Pini was among them, even after having spent ten years in that hell and always with the hope of getting out or die fighting until his last breath if it was no longer possible. But he had not taken into account the sickness that was eating him away and would end up annihilating his entire will, all his energy and then—too late.

I am the only one from that time lucky enough to have survived and to have managed to get free, which allows me to write these lines that are an accurate account, I guarantee, of part of a life lived in that cesspool.

At every opportunity the anarchist comrades there, mindful of their personal dignity and of the respect of their convictions, through their upright behavior in every situation knew how to impress their executioners, who were surprised that in such adversity men held their heads high like that. They could have been hated, but they were forced to be respected—except for a few deserters whom I will talk about later, Ortiz, Placeau, etc. But they were never sincere comrades with firm convictions, just snobs and dilettantes.

Seven years after what happened, I managed to gain this false freedom. But as far as Pini, before he died he might have regretted our lack of resolve when we had plenty of it and after that failure he resolved to take revenge for our escape plan and for all the injustices, humiliations, and degradations that we had suffered since our arrest. Today I regret it, seeing the automaton life that I lead. In the penal colony it was an active life in that constant struggle against our persecutors, spitting our contempt and our disgust in their faces, in the face of their villainies and vileness.

For morale, what satisfaction?

After giving up so much and putting up with such an existence in the hope of seeing my companion again, whom I adored, as much as to continue the fight, I finally saw my loved one after eighteen years. But alas! The love that she had shown me in her letters had been extinguished a long time before ...

End of the first part.

If my sight, which is getting weaker and weaker, and my health, which is also much worse, allow me, I will continue the second part.

❖　❖　❖

[The French manuscript stops here. The remaining pages were lost. The Italian edition goes on for another four hundred pages, covering the last seven years of Duval's life in the penal colony and his escape in April 1901. It is mostly recounting the same story as before, the same monotony, the same disappointed hopes, the same humiliations, etc.

The following was retranslated from the Italian and appeared in the anarchist paper L'En-Dehors:]

Despite the insistence of Garnier, who did not want to postpone the duty to avenge the murder of Briens [by the guard Mosca on October 1, 1894], the comrades on Saint Joseph had decided, for reasons that would be too long and unnecessary to discuss here, to put it off, at least for the moment. The hour would come when the "duty" could be accomplished with more adequate means and with an otherwise far-reaching, prosperous success.

On Sunday morning, October 21, while everyone was washing up on the seashore, the Internal Service orderly went to summon the deportee Malastre, who was bathing. No one paid any attention to it. They knew that Malastre secretly mended the guards' clothes for a few packs of tobacco or some glasses of tafia. But since he was dawdling in the sea, the guard yelled at him from the beach, "Hurry up, Malastre, Mosca is leaving tomorrow in the dinghy for Maroni and wants to have his clothes fixed up."

His fellow inmates looked at him squarely in the face and while a bitter reproach burst out of Garnier's blazing looks, there was the same grief in all the souls. That bastard was leaving scot-free and unpunished for the murder of Briens.

They knew that the original plan was no longer possible after Plista's ratting, but anyway they agreed that they should not let that blood thirsty rogue get off. And after long, hard discussions they decided unanimously that during the first round Simon, Thiervoz, Garnier, Meyrueis, Léauthier, Chevenet, Boasi, Lebeau, Marpaux, and Mazarguil, who were all in the same barrack, would kick over the lamp, charge the slave drivers and the foremen, throw them to the ground, take away their weapons and keys and go let the comrades out of the other barracks.

The screws should certainly have been on their guard after Plista's spying, but since taking the round by surprise was not among the plans that Plista had sold to the slave driver Bonafai, the undertaking still had a great chance of success.

And it was attempted. Boubou, the black foreman, had barely raised the lamp when he came on the round before the guard Crétallaz, when a handful of the most determined men rushed upon him in a flash, riddling him with stab wounds. The guard Mosca, who wisely stayed in the doorway, shot his gun blindly, hitting Garnier in the forehead, dropping him dead on the ground, and then tried to make a run for it to catch up with the foreman Boubou who had managed to slip away in the confusion and run out to inform the Internal Service about the uprising.

However, Thiervoz was watching Mosca and pounced on him like a tiger, disarming him, throwing him to the ground and stabbing him half a dozen times in the side.

During this time, Simon, who was armed with a gun taken from the guard Crétallaz, went from barrack to barrack to break open the doors and collect the handful of willing insurgents, of which there were plenty among the deportees and the comrades who were scattered throughout the cabins. In a confrontation with the guard Dard, Simon was wounded in the hand, but two foremen fell without getting back up.

The Internal Service was awakened by Boubou's yelling and the repeated echoes of gunfire. Commandant Bonafai organized the crackdown, calling for the seamen without delay, who were sent and unloaded that very night, drunk like pigs and unleashed everywhere with the express orders to show no mercy—useless advice for that bunch of fatheads.

[The rebellion was quashed. Twelve convicts were killed, as well as two foremen and two guards. Girier was held mainly responsible, though no witnesses supported it. He died less than three years later in solitary confinement. His case provoked one of the first public criticisms of the penal colony in France.]

# Chapter 12
# Never Go to the Penal Colony

[Letter to Auguste Liard-Courtois, pardoned on December 24, 1899, and returned to France. *Après le bagne*, p. 162]

## Saint Laurent du Maroni, August 18, 1900

My dear Auguste,

I haven't received the books that you said you'd sent me, but I received the charming letter that you addressed to Mr. Director in which you offered your services to me and that I willingly accept because my situation is not good. I can tell you that I have never had as much rage in my heart as I have for the past month being here, seeing the way in which they have deceived me.

Ah! I'm very sorry that you deposited that hundred francs and that I've heaped up these years of suffering to obtain such a result ... Because I'm telling you that the concession is the biggest hoax that exists. There are some raised to concessions who for eighteen months or two years or longer have been waiting for their cases to be built in order to leave on concession.

As for me, my lot has not yet been chosen. My report has not yet been made.

As you can see, there was no need to make such a fuss and to make so many promises just to see me unhappier than I have ever been in the penal colony. If this is the improvement that they think I'm going to accept, they're wrong because I'm at the end of my rope, I've had enough, enough of these dirty tricks …

A few days after I got here, they sent me to Saint Maurice, a new camp where there are a few who were raised to concessions. It's the unhealthiest place in all of Maroni. Men drop like flies from the really awful fevers; there are really noxious fits in that place.

Seeing this I protested right away, saying that it was not the place promised to me, that at the end of fourteen years I was being sent to a place that was far too unhealthy in order to get rid of me. The Commandant sent me back to Saint Laurent fourteen days later. Furthermore, the camp has been terminated since yesterday due to the sickness.

That, dear friend, is the situation in Maroni (which is no longer what you knew). The town has grown, but the misery there is much greater than in your time because of the number of freedmen hit by the ban and the companions who come down from Saint Jean every minute.

In your time, a convict didn't do a chore for anybody without getting paid. Today, there are so many hands in the pie that many freedmen and their companions work for merchants for nothing but food. There are some who are paid ten or fifteen francs a month! Those who work for the district earn two francs a day. In the end, for all these poor men the situation is deplorable and if nothing stops it, the further it goes, the worse it will get.

Under these conditions, you have to understand that the situation of those being granted concessions is not too great and what's the future!

At the moment there are four of us in irons competing to be granted concessions. And like for those who already are in such a situation, it's only misery that awaits us!

For our women it's the same thing, given the number of women leaving the convent as companions. Therefore, for my companion's work, like for mine, it will be total exploitation and misery. And I have urged her not to make the mistake of coming here, at least for the time being ... For that, I hope you will talk her out of it if she still demands to come.

For the rural concession that is given in Saint Maurice or even in the bush around Saint Laurent, there are constant fevers and a quick death. I see these poor country folk; with a few exceptions it makes you sad to see their doomed faces.

Dear friend, if you receive my letter too late, when my companion has made the necessary steps to come join me and she has to leave, I'm counting on you to help her understand the situation of those granted concessions (which I'm sure they are ignorant of in high places) and that under such conditions they cannot make her leave.

I hope you will answer me right away on receiving this letter to let me know that you got it ...

Give my best to all our friends and tell them that although I cannot be there in person with them, I'm there in my heart. Trust, dear friend, in my eternal friendship and gratitude.

Clément Duval

❖   ❖   ❖

[From the National Archives, Colonies series H 1286:]
Saint Laurent du Maroni.
Duval Clément, mle 21551551, concessionnaire.
March 30, 1901.

Governor,

I have just been informed by the High Commandant of Maroni about the denial of my companion's demand to come join me in order to share my exile.

The reason alleged by the Minister is "disagreeable information about the morality of Duval's wife."

Such a motive was so unexpected by me that I was not only upset but very surprised.

Governor, here is why.

I have been here for fourteen years and given my temperament and the independence of my character, I had to make superhuman efforts to accept such a wretched existence. And this because I was sustained by the advice and friendship of a spouse whom I love and whom after fourteen years of promises I hope to see again.

Today when we are ready to reach our goal, in compensation for so many efforts, so many years of moral suffering, etc., all is lost.

However, after the conduct upheld by my companion with respect to me, I must conclude that there is an error. The sincerity of the person in charge of gathering information must have been caught off guard and therefore the Minister as well.

For, Governor, is it the act of an immoral woman whose husband has been sentenced to hard labor for life to write to him for fourteen years without ever missing a letter? And letters full of affection and encouragement.

I think this is unheard of in the annals of the penal colony ...

Is it the act of an immoral woman to go twenty times to the Ministry to remind them of the promises that they made to her to attain her desire to join her husband in this land of exile despite all the efforts that I made to dissuade her, fearing the disastrous consequences of the climate to her health?

Is it the act of an immoral woman to work sixteen hours a day to earn her living?

Besides, since I have many friends, I would certainly have been informed about this immorality. To prove the contrary I am attaching a recent letter of a friend who, after his five-year sentence of hard labor was done, managed to return to France and go see this poor woman.

Please excuse, Governor, the length and rambling of this letter, but unfortunately you can understand in what state of mind such a deception has put me.

Nevertheless, I think that I must face up to adversity, as cruel as it may be, especially not losing the hope of seeing her who is so dear to me, only however, if a counter-investigation is conducted, which I hope will produce a favorable result.

❊   ❊   ❊

[Coded dispatch from Cayenne received in Paris on 4/24/1901:] The deportee Duval 21551 escaped Maroni April 14 after notification of refused authorization to let his wife come.

❊   ❊   ❊

[Duval escaped in a boat with eight others—difficulties on the high seas for inexperienced seamen, hunger, cold, coastal navigation in countries teeming with reunited escapees looking secretly for work. In British Guiana he wrote to Jean Grave to ask for money. From Georgetown to Saint Lucia, then to San Juan, Puerto Rico. In 1903 he was welcomed by the French and Italian anarchists in New York. He faced many difficulties there, not the least of which was that his companion Louise joined him, but things did not work out and she returned to France. He could never bring himself to believe that she was unfaithful and did not live only for him. In the last part of his memoir he writes:]

I remember what a convict told me one day, a guy named Goubau, sentenced to eight years of hard labor, who disembarked in the Salvation Islands, on Royal Island, and during the time he was there we had some nice conversations together. He came to say hello to me from comrade Rieffel, a former editor of the anarchist newspaper *Terre et Liberté*. For one or more of his articles or those of his collaborators he was sentenced in absentia to two or three years in prison. He returned to France and appealed against the decision, I think. That's when he was in custody with Goubau who was awaiting a sentence of hard labor.

Rieffel said to him, "You will undoubtedly see Duval. Give him my best and tell him that in his adversity there should be comfort in knowing that the comrades who knew him have the fondest memories of him. (This was so nice to hear that I was really moved by it.) Also tell him not to worry about his companion, she doesn't deserve it."

That hurt me a lot and I figured she was misjudged and unappreciated by the comrades.

❖   ❖   ❖

I forgot to say while I was in the country with Del ... that a comrade informed me of the death of Allmayer in Maroni.

I had one regret, which was that he had not come while I was there in order to have the satisfaction of killing the little fiend myself. Would I have done it? Would I not have been so cowardly as to let him live? Would I not have been stopped by circumstances that I would have considered more important, so as to excuse this cowardliness to let such a wretch remain alive? Anyway, he's dead, so much the better.

It was different when later in New York I learned about the death of comrade Pini [on June 8, 1903] from the newspapers. Having known him to be dignified in adversity, I wrote a funeral oration for a libertarian newspaper about what I felt. Did they not want to print it? Did it never arrive in the mail? I have no idea.

What I can say today in writing these lines is that he was wrong to accept the concessions in the Islands and not to have come join me in Maroni where I was waiting for him. And I only escaped when there was no more hope of us doing it together. He died ten years after his internment in the Salvation Islands, bearing that miserable existence with dignity and always with the same hope. He figured that when he could no longer stand it, he would act and make them pay dearly for the humiliations and all the evil that they had done to him, as well as to his comrades. But he did not take into account the exhaustion and the sickness that destroyed his entire will and sapped all his energy—and then, too late.

Our lords and masters and their lackeys see us go out like that one after the other, rage in our hearts, regrets to have not done better (which they are unaware of). Also, as long as they are not content with mere threats, they will laugh. If only torrents of ink and a rain of curses would cover them with anathema … Alas! As long as it stops there, they will revel in peace and become more and more arrogant.

All the governments, no matter what they may be, persecute us more and more. They themselves are just the flunkeys of finance, mocking our threats. Do not forget that [Marquis de] Gallifet, who had thousands of Parisians shot, died in his bed after being Minister of War alongside the socialist [Alexandre] Millerand who later became his successor. Bah! What an insult to the people! So, when will they become aware of their cowardliness and their spinelessness?

Poor Pini, I knew your hope, your courage, your physical and moral suffering and I urge the comrades who did not know you to hold you in the fondest remembrance.

Later a new grief was added to the last: the death of comrade Théodule Meunier a year or two afterward, I don't remember [July 25, 1907]. Since I had left the Salvation Islands, I had no news about this good and brave comrade who was so dignified in adversity and by his upright behavior could make an impression on the executioners. I did get some news here through some comrades who were responsible for making a collection for him. The news was vague. I wrote and received no answer from the (freed) addressee to whom the letter was sent.

Later I met an escapee here whom I had known in the Salvation Islands (Saint Joseph). Although he was very young when he arrived, only twenty years old, he was serious, discreet, and courageous. While I was on Saint Joseph he tried to get away with two comrades, Oliveira and a second whose name escapes me. They failed. He was sent to Camp Charvein as an incorrigible.

Meunier, through his demands to be sent to the continent, got himself classed to the works in Maroni. It seems his joy was indescribable, considering the hope he had of escaping. He tried, but he was watched so closely that it was impossible for him to make the preparations by himself. Ah! If only I were still there! I probably would have been able to do nothing for him, but some men who knew me and respected me could have done something. As it was there were some old ex-convicts who did not know Meunier. As a result of several failures he was sent to Camp Charvein as an incorrigible, glad not to have been sent off to the Salvation Islands. He met up with this convict Adrien and the two of them decided to split from the camp at the first opportunity. One morning, it came. But they were seen by an Arab foreman armed with a big, hardwood club who set out after them. Adrien had a head start on Meunier, but when he saw that he was going to be caught by the Arab, he went back and just when the foreman was about to bludgeon him with his club (which could have killed Meunier), he took his machete and struck him such a blow on the arm that it was almost cut off. And they had to amputate it right away.

They slipped away again, but the alarm was sounded and they were after them. Meunier was arrested and straightway sent to Maroni where they put him in solitary until the boat left for the Salvation Islands.

Dearly missed comrade, already physically eaten away by the chronic diarrhea contracted because of the lack of care at the beginning of the sickness, with all hope of regaining your lost liberty, your morality ended up killing your body. Since I knew his rebellious nature that resulted from his spirit of justice and his love of humanity, I realize that his final moments had to have been full of sorrow, to die like that, with rage in his heart, not being able to bring justice before dying.

Comrades, let's salute this brave comrade. The best way to prove our respect and fond memory, is to imitate him, even doing better, if possible.

❖  ❖  ❖

Now that I am old and my sight is failing me for certain work, sometimes I meet some stupid, ignorant, authoritative people who make me feel like I suffered less in the State's penal colony than here, for the work. So I will finish by saying to the readers of these pages, especially the comrades:

Comrades,

I have given you an exact account of a life lived in that hell, the penal colony.

I have said pretty much what I was and what I felt before going there.

On leaving I have delivered to you my innermost life so that you might know the outcome, such as no physiologist, no professional psychologist could do since they themselves have not felt the effects of an uncommon life.

That's why I tell you: If there are any among you who can no longer wait, who are tired of always being the wounded, the crushed, etc., who want to bring justice—Comrades, go all the way.

But first think well about it. For, if you show signs of weakness in the hope of seeing your loved ones again, know that it would be very surprising, after so many years away, to find them again as they should be. Maybe, like me, they will criticize and slander you. It will be with great sorrow that you will see that your act or acts have been misunderstood and distorted. In their slandering you will see the best comrades, whom you respect, distance themselves from you and you will be left alone, unappreciated. Except for the joy of not being so by the ones who know you well, who appreciate and respect you. Such is the case for me, which helps me put up with so much bitterness.

Therefore, comrades, if you act, make them kill you on the spot and cut off your head, but never go to the penal colony.

—C. D.

# Biographies

**BRIENS, François, Jean-Marie**

Born in 1863. Member of the Furniture Workers' Union. He circulated his paper *Le Pot à Colle* in Paris. He was convicted in Troyes, with Placide Catineau, for counterfeiting in February 1894 and sentenced to hard labor for life. On October 1, 1894, on Saint Joseph Island, where he had the prison number 26474, he was fatally wounded by the guard Mosca. This murder would unleash a revolt.

**CAILS, Victor**

Born in Nantes in 1858. He was a marine engineer and met Clément Duval in the penal colony, perhaps on several occasions. When he returned to France, he was arrested in 1891 with Liard-Courtois and Régis Meunier and brought before the Assises Court for "distributing publications that incite people to commit murder, pillage and arson," but he had escaped to England. After being arrested in Walsall in January 1892 with a group of anarchists suspected of possession of explosive charges, he spent more than eight years in prison. He was freed in December 1899 and organized an anarchist club in London, became friends with Louise Michel, tried to immigrate to South America but could not find work, then took to the sea again in 1903. He returned to France at an unknown date. The anarchist newspapers reported his death in 1926.

## CASERIO, Sante

Born in Italy in 1873. While working as a baker in Sète, he heard about the execution of Auguste Vaillant and then of Émile Henry, whom President Sadi Carnot refused to pardon. He bought a sword and went to Lyon on train and by foot. On June 28, 1894, Sadi Carnot, on an official visit to Lyon, was stabbed by Caserio crying out "Vive la Révolution! Vive l'Anarchie!" Some patriotic rioters attacked the Italian consulate and looted Italian-run stores. Caserio appeared before the Assises Court of Rhône on August 3, 1894, and took full responsibility for his act. Condemned to death on August 3, he was guillotined on August 16, 1894.

## CATINEAU, Placide.

Born in 1858. In 1889 he was part of a group of anarchist carpenters in Paris. On February 13, 1894, along with François Briens, he was sentenced to hard labor for life for counterfeiting and trying to escape from prison in Troyes in 1893. He was still alive in Guiana in 1899.

## CHENAL, Louis

Born in 1861. Sentenced to eight years of hard labor for breaking and entering and theft, he arrived in Guiana at the beginning of 1894. Subject to the residence rule, he died there in 1925.

## CHEVENET, Benoît

Born in 1864. Roadworker. Sentenced on July 27, 1892, to twelve years of hard labor for stealing dynamite in collusion with Ravachol, Drouhet, Faugoux, and Étiévant. He was killed in the prison revolt in the Salvation Islands on October 22, 1894.

## COURTOIS, Auguste, called Liard-Courtois

Born in 1862. He made his first public speech in Paris in 1888 for the anniversary of the Commune. In 1891, following a meeting in Nantes, he was sentenced in absentia to two years of prison and a 3,000-franc fine. On May 1, 1891, in Fourmies (North), troops fired on a crowd of people killing nine of them. Courtois went to Fourmies and established a libertarian group there. When he was about to be arrested he went to Belgium and then to England. He returned to Lille, Paris, and finally Bordeaux. During a meeting on March 18, 1892, to celebrate the Paris Commune, he gave a speech that got him prosecuted. A little later they arrested him for his speech in Bordeaux. In January 1894, under the false name of Liard, he was charged with falsifying public documents and sentenced to five years of hard labor. Freed on January 27, 1899, he had to live in Cayenne, but he was pardoned of his remaining five years of banishment. He was one of the five convicts defended by the Ligue des Droits de l'Homme along with François Monod, Anthelme Girier, Théodore Lardaux, and Arthur Vautier. In April 1900 he arrived in Le Havre. He published his *Souvenirs du bagne* (Memoir of the Penal Colony) in 1903 and then *Après le bagne* (After the Penal Colony) in 1905. He died in 1918.

## CRESPIN, Joseph

Born in 1852. Sentenced to eight years of hard labor for theft, he had been connected to the anarchists. According to his file, he escaped on March 3, 1894, and was caught on the sixth; escaped on March 25, 1896, and was caught on the twenty-ninth; escaped on October 1, 1896, and caught on the second; escaped January 20, 1897, and caught on March 30; escaped on July 17, 1898, and caught on the eighteenth; escaped on September 24, 1898, and no news from then on. Every escape attempt earned him a long stay in the hole.

## DAVID, Eugène

Sentenced to eight years of hard labor for theft, he managed to escape in 1899 on his ninth attempt. His friend Auguste Ballin, sentenced to twenty years, had also often tried to escape until he finally gave it up in 1903. He died in the penal colony in 1919.

### DEGRAVE, Eugène

Born in Ostende in 1865. With his brother Léon he committed acts of piracy in French Polynesia under the name of "frères Rorique" (Rorique brothers). They were condemned to death in December 1893, but it was commuted to hard labor for life. Léon died on Royal Island in 1898; Eugène was pardoned a year later in 1899. On his return to France he published *Le Bagne* (The Penal Colony)—"It was in the penal colony where I met the most honest men"—and a few articles.

### DREYFUS, Alfred

Born in 1859, died in 1935. Jewish officer convicted of treason in 1894 and sent to Devil's Island in Guiana before being pardoned in 1899 and then vindicated. His trial deeply divided public opinion.

### ETIÉVANT, Georges

Born in 1865. Tried in July 1892 for complicity with Ravachol and sentenced to five years in prison. During his trial he made a speech for his defense that was published and translated several times. After doing his time he collaborated with the *Libertaire*. Following an article entitled "The Rabbit and the Hunter" in no. 103, he was sentenced in absentia to three years in prison in 1897. When he was arrested by police officers he was carrying a sword and a revolver and slightly wounded them. Although he did not kill anyone, he was sentenced to death, but his sentence was commuted to hard labor for life. He was sent to the penal colony in Cayenne and died a year later [February 6, 1900].

### FAUGOUX, Auguste Alfred

Born in 1862. Sentenced on July 27, 1892, to twenty years of hard labor and twenty years of banishment for stealing dynamite in Soisy-sous-Étiolles on the night of February 14 in collusion with Ravachol, Chevenet, Drouhet, and Étiévant. He was sent to Guiana where he would fall sick. Sent to the infirmary on Royal Island, he died of dysentery in November 1894.

## FORET, Jean-Baptiste

Born in 1870. Arrested in 1893 for attempted theft of rabbits, he was sentenced to life for "attempted murder" (during the theft he had wounded a bourgeois who intervened) and was part of the convoy that embarked in Saint-Martin-de-Ré on December 18, 1893, heading for the penal colony in Cayenne. Foret was accused of participating in the revolt of anarchist prisoners but was acquitted in the end. In December 1895 he was in prison on Saint Joseph Island (number 26120). His case was defended by the libertarian press, especially by Séverine. Pardoned, he returned to France in 1901.

## GALLEANI, Luigi

Born in Italy in 1861. Escaped the penal colony of Pantelleria and arrived in the United States in 1901 where he founded newspapers supporting direct action and insurrection. He welcomed Clément Duval whose *Memoir* he translated. He was expelled from the United States in 1919 and returned to Italy where, after several stints in prison, he died in 1931.

## GIRIER, Jean-Baptiste Anthelme Eugène, called "Lorion"

Born in 1869. At thirteen years old he ran away from his parents and was sentenced to eight days in prison for vagrancy. Following an altercation with a police superintendant they locked him up in a reformatory—he got out around the middle of 1886. He found some work in Lyon, but was sent back when his boss learned that was an anarchist. For a speech given in a public meeting he was convicted in absentia on November 12, 1888, to one year in prison. He went to Paris, then to the "Département du Nord"—or Roubaix—where he called himself Lorion. He continued promoting anarchism there and was sentenced to ten years of hard labor and banishment for "rebellion against police officers." In October 1893 Girier was sent to Saint Joseph Island where he would work as a gardener and on November 11 participate with other comrades in a talk for the anniversary of the Chicago martyrs who were hanged on November 11, 1887 (the Haymarket Affair). On July 2, 1894, seventy-five convicts on Saint Joseph Island refused to leave their barracks to go to the work sites. On October 21 and 22 the anarchist prisoners revolted and killed the guard Mosca. Girier, considered "the soul of the plot," was sentenced to death in June 1895. He awaited his execution every morning keeping a diary in the form of letters that he addressed to Monsieur Sévère, his defense attorney who published them in the *Libertaire*. He died on November 16, 1898.

## GRAVE, Jean

Born in 1854, died in 1939. Editor of the papers *La Révolte* and *Les Temps Nouveaux* in Paris, he was one of the main promoters of anarchy in France.

## HENRY, Émile

Born in 1872. On November 8, 1892, the bomb that he had put in front of the Société des Mines de Carmaux in Paris to show his solidarity with the striking miners exploded at the police station on Rue des Bons-Enfants, where it had been transported, and caused a massacre of police officers. Émile Henry left the next day to take refuge in England. On the evening of February 12, 1894, determined to strike at the bourgeoisie, he threw a bomb into the middle of the Café Terminus at the Gare Saint-Lazare in Paris. Around twenty people were wounded; one was killed. Émile Henry fled and was chased by customers and police officers on whom he fired upon with his gun, but who ended up arresting him. He read a powerful statement at his trial that was printed in a number of newspapers. He was guillotined on May 21, 1894.

## HINCELIN, Auguste

Born around 1870. Sentenced to eight years of hard labor after a dozen earlier convictions for theft, vagrancy, and insulting a judge. Acquitted after the revolt of 1894, he was still in Guiana in 1921.

## KROPOTKINE, Pierre

Born in 1842, died in 1921. One of the main theoreticians of anarchy.

## LABORI, Fernand

Born in 1860, died in 1917. He was the defense attorney for Duval, one of his first cases. He went on to defend the anarchist Auguste Vaillant, Captain Dreyfus, and other people in dire straits.

## LEAUTHIER, Léon Jules

Born in 1874. An out-of-work cobbler, he went to Paris in 1893 and when he could not find work he decided to get his revenge. On November 13, 1893, he went into action and wounded a customer at a restaurant who turned out to be a Serbian diplomat and then he gave himself up to the police. He was sentenced on February 23, 1894, to hard labor for life. During the trip to Guiana, he participated in a revolt on board the ship *Ville de Saint Nazaire*. He was killed on October 22, 1894, in the revolt of prisoners on Saint Joseph Island.

## LEBAULT (or LEBEAU), Louis

Born in 1868. Sentenced in 1893 to eight years of hard labor for various thefts. At that time, according to the police, he had no known links with the anarchists. He was killed on October 22, 1894, with a dozen other comrades. According to a police report he was killed "on the rocks bordering the east coast of the island … crying out 'Vive l'anarchie.'"

## LEPIEZ, Léon Auguste

Born in 1870. Typographer. Sentenced to ten years of hard labor in 1892 for attempted arson and defamation of the army, he "admitted his anarchist opinions during the trial." Freed in 1902, he died in Cayenne in 1907.

## MARCHAND, Gustave

Sentenced to life for murder, he was not known as an anarchist. Despite a reputation for bad behavior and attempted escapes, he was offered conditional freedom starting in 1896. He did not get it until 1924 and could not leave Guiana until 1931.

## MARPAUX, Edmond Aubin

Born in 1866. Metal embosser. He attended anarchist meetings organized in Paris. On August 18, 1893, he was arrested for yelling "Vive l'anarchie!" in front of a guardian of the peace who snatched away the posters that Marpaux had put up that very morning. He was released. On November 29 during a fight with police officers, he critically wounded one of them with a knife. He was sentenced to hard labor for life. The police described him as "dishonorable, libertine and debauched, living out of wedlock, a dangerous anarchist, with no means of subsistence." He died on October 22, 1894, during the revolt in the Salvation Islands.

## MARTIN, Pierre

Born in 1856, died in 1916. A devoted and constant propagandist, he could not count all his prison sentences. After the first demonstration on May 1, 1890, in Vienna (Isère, France), he was convicted of being the head of the riots. His years in prison seriously affected his health.

## MEUNIER, Régis

Born in 1864. Former capuchin friar, he was sentenced on July 2, 1891, to one year in prison and a 100-franc fine for inciting to murder and pillage. At the pronouncement of the sentence he cried out "Vive l'anarchie," which earned him another month in prison and another 100-franc fine. Prosecuted for incidents that occurred during a strike, but also for conferences he gave in Limoges and Brest, he was sentenced on May 30, 1894, to seven years of hard labor and ten years of banishment. When his prison time was done, he lived in Saint-Laurent-du-Maroni where he worked in a brickyard for slave wages. He was pardoned by a decree dated June 18, 1901, following efforts made by the Ligue des Droits de l'Homme and returned to France in 1902. He set up again in Brest where he continued promoting anarchism. He died in 1936.

## MEUNIER, Théodule

Born in 1860. The day before the appearance of Ravachol before the Assises Court of Seine, on April 25, 1892, a bomb exploded in the Restaurant Véry killing two people and wounding several others. Théodule Meunier was the perpetrator of the attack as well as that of the Caserne Lobau on March 15, 1892. French police arrested him in London in June 1894. He was tried in Paris on July 26, 1894, saved his neck by denying his guilt, but was sentenced to hard labor for life. From the penal colony he kept in correspondence with Jean Grave. Meunier was hoping for a press campaign to free him, but he died in Cayenne on July 25, 1907. Several escape attempts had failed and his health was battered.

## MEYRUEIS, Henri Pierre

Born in 1865. Sentenced to life for murder. The administration considered him "one of the most violent anarchists" even though he had had no prior convictions. He was killed during the revolt of 1894.

## MICHEL, Louise

Born in 1830, died in 1905. An emblematic figure of the Paris Commune and of anarchism. She was exiled to New Caledonia from 1873 to 1880. In 1883 she was sentenced to prison following a riot in Paris in which the demonstrators had pillaged the bakeries. She continued to make conference tours until the day before she died.

## ORTIZ, Léon (SCHIROKY)

Practicing "individual reclamation" he was prosecuted in August 1894 in the Trial of the Thirty (anarchist theoreticians and supporters of individual reclamation) and sentenced to fifteen years of hard labor. In the penal colony in Cayenne he quickly cut himself off from the anarchist community and strove to get in the good graces of the administration. His sentence was, in fact, commuted and he got back to France in 1898.

## PARIDAËN, Joseph Quintin

Born in 1873. A caster and then salesclerk, he put up revolutionary posters in Le Havre and sold anarchist newspapers in Paris. Sentenced in 1892 to ten years of hard labor for theft. He escaped the penal colony in Guiana in 1904.

## PINI, Vittorio

Born in Italy in 1859. He was already a militant in Italy when he arrived in France in 1886 working as a cobbler in Paris. Around 1887 with his compatriot Luigi Parmeggiani he founded the anarchist group "Gli Intransigenti di Londra e Parigi," advocating and practicing individual reclamation, especially to finance their papers. During a search of his house in June 1889 police found a whole range of weapons, along with the remains of numerous robberies committed in Paris and the countryside. He was sentenced to twenty years of hard labor, which he accepted with the cry "Vive l'Anarchie! À bas les voleurs!" (Long live anarchy! Down with thieves!). His conviction revived the debate in the heart of the anarchist movement about the legitimacy of theft, which began with the trial of Clément Duval. On August 15, 1890, he was sent to the penal colony in Guiana from where he tried to escape twice without success. In 1902 they granted him a remission of three years. He died of illness in the penal colony in December 1903.

## RAVACHOL, François

Born in 1859. Forced to work at the age of eight to help his family, he became an anarchist by a revolt against the injustice of society. To protest the convictions of anarchists after May 1, 1891, he stole dynamite with some comrades and put bombs in judges' houses. He was guillotined on July 11, 1892.

## RECLUS, Elisée

Born in 1830, died in 1905. Geographer and one of the great theoreticians of anarchism, he was one of the few who did not condemn the acts of Duval or Ravachol.

## ROSSIGNOL, Gustave Armand

Police sergeant and then detective. In his *Memoir* he told about the arrest of Duval and in 1900 published a dictionary of slang.

## ROUSSEAU

It was at Rousseau's wine shop, 131 Rue Saint Martin in Paris, that different anarchist groups met in the 1880s: carpenters, cobblers, barbers, waiters. It was also there that was born the "déménageurs à la cloche-de-bois" (Midnight Movers), as well as the Jack-of-all-trades Union and the "Secte des pieds-plats" (Sect of Flatfoots), who lived on expedients in order not to have to work.

## SÉVERINE (pseudonym of Caroline REMY)

Born in 1855, died in 1929. Journalist, feminist, and anarchist, she bravely supported Clément Duval and later Dreyfus, Sacco and Vanzetti, and others.

## SEVOX, Henry

Sentenced to life for murder, in 1885 he was considered "one of the most dangerous men and should never return to France." He managed to escape in 1893.

## SIMON, Charles Achille, called Biscuit and Ravachol II

Born in 1873. Comrade of Ravachol, he was sentenced to life in 1892 for complicity in the assassination attempts. He died on October 23, 1894, in the penal colony in Guiana during the prisoners' revolt. "A hideous little chap whose shriveled face bore the stigmata of all his vices. He did not even have the 'jest' of a vagabond; his habits of awful debauchery had extinguished every gleam of intelligence in him." (Paul Mimande, *Forçats et proscrits*)

## TODD, Charles

Born in London in 1842. He was first sent to the penal colony in New Caledonia. He arrived in Guiana in 1892, sentenced to twenty years of hard labor. After six escape attempts in which he was quickly caught, he finally managed to escape in 1905.

## TORTELIER, Joseph

Born in 1854, died in 1925. Carpenter and with Clément Duval a member of the group La Panthère des Batignolles (the Batignolles is a quarter in Paris), he made himself the propagandist for the general strike in countless meetings in France, England, and the United States.

## VAILLANT, Auguste

Born in 1861. After a life of political activism and poverty, he threw a bomb full of nails into the Chamber of Deputies in Paris on December 9, 1893. It only wounded a few men. He claimed responsibility for his act the next day and was sentenced to death after a short trial. He was guillotined on February 5, 1894.

**Biographies taken from:** *Dictionnaire international des militants anarchistes* (http://militants-anarchistes.info).

# Bibliography

## Archives

Centre International de Recherches sur l'Anarchisme (CIRA), Lausanne:
The manuscript of the Mémoires of Clément Duval and its complete tran-
scription, as well as some supplementary documents are held here.

Archives Nationales d'Outre-Mer, Aix-en-Provence; Colonies, série H.

## Periodicals

*L'Adunata dei Refrattari*, Newark, NJ, 1922–1971

*Le Cri du Peuple*, Paris, 23 and 31 January 1887

*Cronaca Sovversiva*, Barre, VT, 1903–1919

*L'En Dehors*, Paris-Orléans, 1926–1935

*Le Libertaire*, Paris, since 1895

*Le Père Peinard*, Paris, 1889–1899

*La Révolte*, Paris, 1889–1890

*Le Semeur*, Caen, 1935

*Le Voleur*, illustrated magazine, Paris, 1886–1887

# Books

Avrich, Paul. *Sacco and Vanzetti: The Anarchist Background*. Princeton: Princeton University Press, 1991.

Degrave, Eugène. *Affaire Rorique, le bagne*. Paris: P.V. Stock, 1902.

Deveze, Michel. *Cayenne, déportés et bagnards*. Paris: Julliard, 1965.

Duval, Clément. *Memorie autobiografiche*. Newark, NJ: Biblioteca de L'Adunata dei refrattari, 1929.

Duval, Clément. *Moi, Clément Duval, bagnard et anarchiste*. Edited by Marianne Enckell. Paris: Edition Ouvrières, 1991.

Galleani, Luigi. *Aneliti e singuli*, Newark, NJ: Biblioteca de L'Adunata dei refrattari, 1935.

Galleani, Luigi. *Faccia a faccia col nemico, cronache giudiziarie dell'anarchismo militante*. Boston: Gruppo Autonomo, 1914.

Hughes, Robert. *The Fatal Shore: A History of the Transportation of Convicts to Australia, 1787–1868*. London: Collins Harvill, 1987.

Krakovitch, Odile. *Les femmes bagnardes*. Paris: O. Orban, 1990.

Liard-Courtois, Auguste. *Souvenirs du bagne*. Paris: Charpentier et Fasquelle, 1903.

Liard-Courtois, Auguste. *Après le bagne*. Paris: Charpentier et Fasquelle, 1905.

Maitron, Jean, *Le Mouvement anarchiste en France*. Paris: Société universitaire d'éditions et de librairie, 1955.

Maitron, Jean, ed. *Dictionnaire biographique du mouvement ouvrier français, 1871–1914*, vols. 10–15. Paris: Editions ouvrières, 1972–1977.

Reinach, Joseph. *Rapport sur le cas de cinq détenus des îles du Salut*. Paris: P.V. Stock, 1899.

Reclus, Elisée. *Correspondance*, vol. 3. Paris: Schleicher, 1926.

# Acknowledgments

A special thanks goes out to Marianne Enckell for all her contributions, support, suggestions, and expertise to help bring this book to fruition.

And of course we wouldn't be reading this witness if it weren't for PM Press. Thanks to Ramsey, Craig, Jonathan, Gregory, Romy, and the folks there for keeping these voices alive.

**Michael Shreve** has taught Greek, Latin, French, Spanish, English, and classical civilization courses in universities and private schools in the United States, Canada, Lebanon, Mexico, Malaysia, and France over the past fifteen years. He has published dozens of translations, both nonfiction and fiction, including works by Voltaire, Jean Meslier, Jacques Barbéri, Pierre Pelot, John Antoine Nau, and many others. He currently lives in Reykjavik, Iceland. He can be found on the web at www.michaelshreve.wordpress.com.

**Marianne Enckell** published the first French version of Duval's memoirs: *Moi, Clement Duval, bagnard et anarchiste*. She is also a translator, and librarian-archivist at the Centre international de recherches sur l'anarchisme (http://www.cira.ch/) in Lausanne, Switzerland.

# ABOUT PM PRESS

PM Press was founded at the end of 2007 by a small collection of folks with decades of publishing, media, and organizing experience. PM Press co-conspirators have published and distributed hundreds of books, pamphlets, CDs, and DVDs. Members of PM have founded enduring book fairs, spearheaded victorious tenant organizing campaigns, and worked closely with bookstores, academic conferences, and even rock bands to deliver political and challenging ideas to all walks of life. We're old enough to know what we're doing and young enough to know what's at stake.

We seek to create radical and stimulating fiction and non-fiction books, pamphlets, T-shirts, visual and audio materials to entertain, educate and inspire you. We aim to distribute these through every available channel with every available technology — whether that means you are seeing anarchist classics at our bookfair stalls; reading our latest vegan cookbook at the café; downloading geeky fiction e-books; or digging new music and timely videos from our website.

PM Press is always on the lookout for talented and skilled volunteers, artists, activists and writers to work with. If you have a great idea for a project or can contribute in some way, please get in touch.

**PM Press**
**PO Box 23912**
**Oakland, CA 94623**
**www.pmpress.org**

# FRIENDS OF PM PRESS

These are indisputably momentous times—the financial system is melting down globally and the Empire is stumbling. Now more than ever there is a vital need for radical ideas.

In the four years since its founding—and on a mere shoestring—PM Press has risen to the formidable challenge of publishing and distributing knowledge and entertainment for the struggles ahead. With over 175 releases to date, we have published an impressive and stimulating array of literature, art, music, politics, and culture. Using every available medium, we've succeeded in connecting those hungry for ideas and information to those putting them into practice.

*Friends of PM* allows you to directly help impact, amplify, and revitalize the discourse and actions of radical writers, filmmakers, and artists. It provides us with a stable foundation from which we can build upon our early successes and provides a much-needed subsidy for the materials that can't necessarily pay their own way. You can help make that happen—and receive every new title automatically delivered to your door once a month—by joining as a Friend of PM Press. And, we'll throw in a free T-shirt when you sign up.

Here are your options:
- **$25 a month** Get all books and pamphlets plus 50% discount on all webstore purchases
- **$40 a month** Get all PM Press releases (including CDs and DVDs) plus 50% discount on all webstore purchases
- **$100 a month** Superstar—Everything plus PM merchandise, free downloads, and 50% discount on all webstore purchases

For those who can't afford $25 or more a month, we're introducing **Sustainer Rates** at $15, $10 and $5. Sustainers get a free PM Press T-shirt and a 50% discount on all purchases from our website.

Your Visa or Mastercard will be billed once a month, until you tell us to stop. Or until our efforts succeed in bringing the revolution around. Or the financial meltdown of Capital makes plastic redundant. Whichever comes first.

"Demanding the Impossible is the book I always recommend when asked—as I often am—for something on the history and ideas of anarchism."
—NOAM CHOMSKY

## Demanding the Impossible
### A History of Anarchism

Peter Marshall
ISBN: 978-1-60486-064-1
$28.95 • 840 pages

Navigating the broad "river of anarchy," from Taoism to Situationism, from Ranters to Punk rockers, from individualists to communists, from anarcho-syndicalists to anarcha-feminists, *Demanding the Impossible* is an authoritative and lively study of a widely misunderstood subject. It explores the key anarchist concepts of society and the state, freedom and equality, authority and power and investigates the successes and failure of the anarchist movements throughout the world. While remaining sympathetic to anarchism, it presents a balanced and critical account. It covers not only the classic anarchist thinkers, such as Godwin, Proudhon, Bakunin, Kropotkin, Reclus, and Emma Goldman, but also other libertarian figures, such as Nietzsche, Camus, Gandhi, Foucault, and Chomsky. No other book on anarchism covers so much so incisively.

In this updated edition, a new epilogue examines the most recent developments, including "post-anarchism" and "anarcho-primitivism" as well as the anarchist contribution to the peace, green, and "Global Justice" movements.

*Demanding the Impossible* is essential reading for anyone wishing to understand what anarchists stand for and what they have achieved. It will also appeal to those who want to discover how anarchism offers an inspiring and original body of ideas and practices which is more relevant than ever in the twenty-first century.

"Attractively written and fully referenced … bound to be the standard history."
—Colin Ward, *Times Educational Supplement*

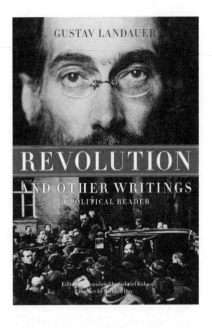

# Revolution and Other Writings
## A Political Reader

Gustav Landauer •Edited and
translated by Gabriel Kuhn
ISBN: 978-1-60486-054-2
$26.95 • 360 Pages

"Landauer is the most important agitator of the radical and revolutionary movement in the entire country." This is how Gustav Landauer is described in a German police file from 1893. Twenty-six years later, Landauer would die at the hands of reactionary soldiers who overthrew the Bavarian Council Republic, a three-week attempt to realize libertarian socialism amidst the turmoil of post-World War I Germany. It was the last chapter in the life of an activist, writer, and mystic who Paul Avrich calls "the most influential German anarchist intellectual of the twentieth century."

This is the first comprehensive collection of Landauer writings in English. It includes one of his major works, *Revolution*, thirty additional essays and articles, and a selection of correspondence. The texts cover Landauer's entire political biography, from his early anarchism of the 1890s to his philosophical reflections at the turn of the century, the subsequent establishment of the Socialist Bund, his tireless agitation against the war, and the final days among the revolutionaries in Munich. Additional chapters collect Landauer's articles on radical politics in the U.S. and Mexico, and illustrate the scope of his writing with texts on corporate capital, language, education, and Judaism. The book includes an extensive introduction, commentary, and bibliographical information, compiled by the editor and translator Gabriel Kuhn as well as a preface by Richard Day.

"At once an individualist and a socialist, a Romantic and a mystic, a militant and an advocate of passive resistance ... He was also the most influential German anarchist intellectual of the twentieth century."
—Paul Avrich, author of *Anarchist Voices*

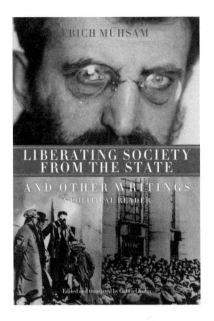

# Liberating Society from the State and Other Writings
## A Political Reader

Erich Mühsam • Edited and translated by Gabriel Kuhn

ISBN: 978-1-60486-055-9

$26.95 • 320 pages

Erich Mühsam (1878–1934), poet, bohemian, revolutionary, is one of Germany's most renowned and influential anarchists. Born into a middle-class Jewish family, he challenged the conventions of bourgeois society at the turn of the century, engaged in heated debates on the rights of women and homosexuals, and traveled Europe in search of radical communes and artist colonies. He was a primary instigator of the ill-fated Bavarian Council Republic in 1919, and held the libertarian banner high during a Weimar Republic that came under increasing threat by right-wing forces. In 1933, four weeks after Hitler's ascension to power, Mühsam was arrested in his Berlin home. He spent the last sixteen months of his life in detention and died in the Oranienburg Concentration Camp in July 1934.

Mühsam wrote poetry, plays, essays, articles, and diaries. His work unites a burning desire for individual liberation with anarcho-communist convictions, and bohemian strains with syndicalist tendencies. The body of his writings is immense, yet hardly any English translations exist. This collection presents not only *Liberating Society from the State: What is Communist Anarchism?*, Mühsam's main political pamphlet and one of the key texts in the history of German anarchism, but also some of his best-known poems, unbending defenses of political prisoners, passionate calls for solidarity with the lumpenproletariat, recollections of the utopian community of Monte Verità, debates on the rights of homosexuals and women, excerpts from his journals, and essays contemplating German politics and anarchist theory as much as Jewish identity and the role of intellectuals in the class struggle.

An appendix documents the fate of Zenzl Mühsam, who, after her husband's death, escaped to the Soviet Union where she spent twenty years in Gulag camps.

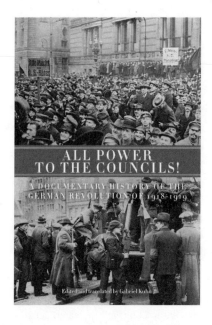

# All Power to the Councils!

A Documentary History of the German Revolution of 1918–1919

Edited and translated by Gabriel Kuhn

ISBN: 978-1-60486-111-2
$26.95 • 352 Pages

The German Revolution erupted out of the ashes of World War I, triggered by mutinying sailors refusing to be sacrificed in the final carnage of the war. While the Social Democrats grabbed power, radicals across the country rallied to establish a communist society under the slogan "All Power to the Councils!" The Spartacus League launched an uprising in Berlin, council republics were proclaimed in Bremen and Bavaria, and workers' revolts shook numerous German towns. Yet in an act that would tragically shape the course of history, the Social Democratic government crushed the rebellions with the help of right-wing militias, paving the way for the ill-fated Weimar Republic—and ultimately the ascension of the Nazis.

This definitive documentary history collects manifestos, speeches, articles, and letters from the German Revolution—Rosa Luxemburg, the Revolutionary Stewards, and Gustav Landauer amongst others—introduced and annotated by the editor. Many documents, such as the anarchist Erich Mühsam's comprehensive account of the Bavarian Council Republic, are presented here in English for the first time. The volume also includes materials from the Red Ruhr Army that repelled the reactionary Kapp Putsch in 1920 and the communist bandits that roamed Eastern Germany until 1921. *All Power to the Councils!* provides a dynamic and vivid picture of a time of great hope and devastating betrayal.

> "Gabriel Kuhn's excellent volume illuminates a profound global revolutionary moment, in which brilliant ideas and debates lit the sky."
> —Marcus Rediker, author of *Villains of all Nations* and *The Slave Ship*

# The CNT in the Spanish Revolution

Written by José Peirats
Introduction by Chris Ealham
Volume 1
ISBN: 978-1-60486-207-2
$28.00 • 432 pages
Volume 2
ISBN: 978-1-60486-208-9
$22.95 • 312 pages
Volume 3
ISBN: 978-1-60486-209-6
$22.95 • 296 pages

*The CNT in the Spanish Revolution* is the history of one of the most original and audacious, and arguably also the most far-reaching, of all the twentieth-century revolutions. It is the history of the giddy years of political change and hope in 1930s Spain, when the so-called "Generation of '36," Peirats' own generation, rose up against the oppressive structures of Spanish society. It is also a history of a revolution that failed, crushed in the jaws of its enemies on both the reformist left and the reactionary right.

José Peirats' account is effectively the official CNT history of the war, passionate, partisan but, above all, intelligent. Its huge sweeping canvas covers all areas of the anarchist experience—the spontaneous militias, the revolutionary collectives, the moral dilemmas occasioned by the clash of revolutionary ideals, and the stark reality of the war effort against Franco and his German Nazi and Italian Fascist allies.

This new edition is carefully indexed in a way that converts the work into a usable tool for historians and makes it much easier for the general reader to dip in with greater purpose and pleasure.

*Volume 2* focuses on the battles raging at both the front and rear guards. Additionally, a biographical chapter, "The Life and Struggles of José Peirats" gives a great deal of insight into this CNT fighter and historian.

*Volume 3* tells of the CNT's last push for the anarchist revolution in Spain, and the crushing defeat of the wide ranging activities of the CNT. An additional chapter surveys "The History of Spanish Anarchism in the English Language."

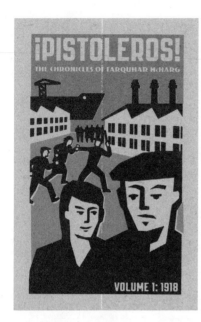

## Pistoleros!
### The Chronicles of Farquhar McHarg - I: 1918

Farquhar McHarg
ISBN: 978-1-60486-401-4
$18.95 • 256 Pages

Barcelona, 1976: Hired gunmen brutally murder a lifelong friend and fellow anarchist, forcing Farquhar McHarg into a race to document an epic history before he too can be silenced. The first volume of his memoirs finds him a Glasgow boy, dropped by chance into Barcelona's revolutionary underworld at the tail end of the great imperialist war of 1914–1918, recruited by Spanish anarchists to act as a go-between with Britain's Secret Service Bureau. McHarg tells of a corrupt and brutal Spanish regime, bent on bringing a rebellious working class back under its heel, and the generous and recklessly idealistic men and women who struggled to transform it after rejecting traditional party politics.

*Pistoleros!* is a thrilling tale of intrigue and romance, and a sweeping inside view of the saboteurs and spies, the capitalists and bold insurrectionaries of Spain's bloody past.

"Written with tremendous brio, this is a passionate and gripping tale of an idealist's coming of age. McHarg's gripping narrative convincingly taps the rich historical seams of intrigue, protest and conflict of an age in which many of the streets of Barcelona became stained with blood."
—Chris Ealham, author of *Anarchism and the City: Revolution and Counter-Revolution in Barcelona, 1898–1937*

"A rare plunge into the dark whirlpool of politics, passion and intrigue that swirled around the docks, bars and tenements of Barcelona in 1918 … *Pistoleros!* is a crack shot that rings out to remind us of times that were less bland."
—Pauline Melville, actress and author of *Shape-Shifter* and *The Ventriloquist's Tale*

## Anarchist Seeds beneath the Snow
### Left-Libertarian Thought and British Writers from William Morris to Colin Ward

David Goodway
ISBN: 978-1-60486-221-8
$24.95 • 448 Pages

From William Morris to Oscar Wilde to George Orwell, left-libertarian thought has long been an important but neglected part of British cultural and political history. In *Anarchist Seeds beneath the Snow*, David Goodway seeks to recover and revitalize that indigenous anarchist tradition. This book succeeds as simultaneously a cultural history of left-libertarian thought in Britain and a demonstration of the applicability of that history to current politics. Goodway argues that a recovered anarchist tradition could—and should—be a touchstone for contemporary political radicals. Moving seamlessly from Aldous Huxley and Colin Ward to the war in Iraq, this challenging volume will energize leftist movements throughout the world.

"Goodway outlines with admirable clarity the many variations in anarchist thought. By extending outwards to left-libertarians he takes on even greater diversity."
 —Sheila Rowbotham, *Red Pepper*

"A splendid survey of 'left-libertarian thought' in this country, it has given me hours of delight and interest. Though it is very learned, it isn't dry. Goodway's friends in the awkward squad (especially William Blake) are both stimulating and comforting companions in today's political climate."
 —A.N. Wilson, *Daily Telegraph*

## The Floodgates of Anarchy

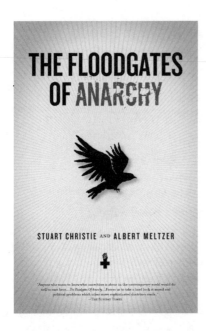

Stuart Christie and Albert Meltzer
ISBN: 978-1-60486-105-1
$15.95 • 144 pages

The floodgates holding back anarchy are constantly under strain. The liberal would ease the pressure by diverting some of the water; the conservative would shore up the dykes, the totalitarian would construct a stronger dam.

But is anarchy a destructive force? The absence of government may alarm the authoritarian, but is a liberated people really its own worst enemy—or is the true enemy of mankind, as the anarchists claim, the means by which he is governed? Without government the world could manage to end exploitation and war. Anarchy should not be confused with weak, divided or manifold government. As Christie and Meltzer point out, only with the total abolition of government can society develop in freedom.

"Anyone who wants to know what anarchism is about in the contemporary world would do well to start here. *The Floodgates of Anarchy* forces us to take a hard look at moral and political problems which other more sophisticated doctrines evade."
— *The Sunday Times*

"A lucid exposition of revolutionary anarchist theory."
— *Peace News*

"Coming from a position of uncompromising class struggle and a tradition that includes many of our exemplary anarchist militants *The Floodgates of Anarchy* has a power and directness sadly missing from some contemporary anarchist writing. It is exciting to see it back in print, ready for a new generation to read."
— Barry Pateman, Associate Editor, The Emma Goldman Papers, University of California at Berkeley

# Anarchism and Education

A Philosophical Perspective

Judith Suissa
ISBN: 978-1-60486-114-3
$19.95 • 184 pages

While there have been historical accounts of the anarchist school movement, there has been no systematic work on the philosophical underpinnings of anarchist educational ideas—until now.

*Anarchism and Education* offers a philosophical account of the neglected tradition of anarchist thought on education. Although few anarchist thinkers wrote systematically on education, this analysis is based largely on a reconstruction of the educational thought of anarchist thinkers gleaned from their various ethical, philosophical, and popular writings. Primarily drawing on the work of the nineteenth century anarchist theorists such as Bakunin, Kropotkin, and Proudhon, the book also covers twentieth century anarchist thinkers such as Noam Chomsky, Paul Goodman, Daniel Guerin, and Colin Ward.

This original work will interest philosophers of education and educationalist thinkers as well as those with a general interest in anarchism.

> "This is an excellent book that deals with important issues through the lens of anarchist theories and practices of education ... The book tackles a number of issues that are relevant to anybody who is trying to come to terms with the philosophy of education."
> —*Higher Education Review*

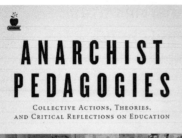

# Anarchist Pedagogies
Collective Actions, Theories, and Critical Reflections on Education

Edited by Robert H. Haworth
Afterword by Allan Antliff
ISBN: 978-1-60486-484-7
$24.95 • 352 Pages

Education is a challenging subject for anarchists. Many are critical about working within a state-run education system that is embedded in hierarchical, standardized, and authoritarian structures. Numerous individuals and collectives envision the creation of counter-publics or alternative educational sites as possible forms of resistance, while other anarchists see themselves as "saboteurs" within the public arena—believing that there is a need to contest dominant forms of power and educational practices from multiple fronts. Of course, if anarchists agree that there are no blueprints for education, the question remains, in what dynamic and creative ways can we construct non-hierarchical, anti-authoritarian, mutual, and voluntary educational spaces?

Contributors to the edited volume *Anarchist Pedagogies: Collective Actions, Theories, and Critical Reflections on Education* engage readers in important and challenging issues in the area of anarchism and education. From Francisco Ferrer's modern schools in Spain and the Work People's College in the United States, to contemporary actions in developing "free skools" in the U.K. and Canada, to direct action education such as learning to work as a "street medic" in the protests against neoliberalism, the contributors illustrate the importance of developing complex connections between educational theories and collective actions. Anarchists, activists, and critical educators should take these educational experiences seriously as they offer invaluable examples for potential teaching and learning environments outside of authoritarian and capitalist structures. Major themes in the volume include: learning from historical anarchist experiments in education, ways that contemporary anarchists create dynamic and situated learning spaces, and finally, critically reflecting on theoretical frameworks and educational practices. Contributors include: David Gabbard, Jeffery Shantz, Isabelle Fremeaux & John Jordan, Abraham P. DeLeon, Elsa Noterman, Andre Pusey, Matthew Weinstein, Alex Khasnabish, and many others.

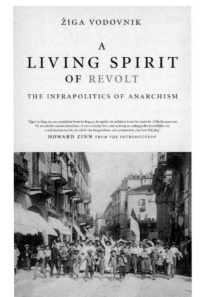

# A Living Spirit of Revolt
## The Infrapolitics of Anarchism

Žiga Vodovnik

Introduction by Howard Zinn

ISBN: 978-1-60486-523-3

$15.95 • 232 Pages

"The great contribution of Žiga Vodovnik is that his writing rescues anarchism from its dogma, its rigidity, its isolation from the majority of the human race. He reveals the natural anarchism of our everyday lives, and in doing so, enlarges the possibilities for a truly human society, in which our imaginations, our compassion, can have full play." —Howard Zinn, author of *A People's History of the United States*, from the Introduction

At the end of the nineteenth century, the network of anarchist collectives represented the first-ever global antisystemic movement and the very center of revolutionary tumult. In this groundbreaking and magisterial work, Žiga Vodovnik establishes that anarchism today is not only the most revolutionary current but, for the first time in history, the only one left. According to the author, many contemporary theoretical reflections on anarchism marginalize or neglect to mention the relevance of the anarchy of everyday life. Given this myopic (mis)conception of its essence, we are still searching for anarchism in places where the chances of actually finding it are the smallest.

"Žiga Vodovnik has made a fresh and original contribution to our understanding of anarchism, by unearthing its importance for the New England Transcendentalists and their impact on radical politics in America. *A Living Spirit of Revolt* is interesting, relevant and is sure to be widely read and enjoyed."
—Uri Gordon, author of *Anarchy Alive: Anti-Authoritarian Politics from Practice to Theory*

## Anarchy Comics
### The Complete Collection

Edited by Jay Kinney
ISBN: 978-1-60486-531-8
$20.00 • 224 Pages

*Anarchy Comics: The Complete Collection* brings together the legendary four issues of *Anarchy Comics* (1978–1986), the underground comic that melded anarchist politics with a punk sensibility, producing a riveting mix of satire, revolt, and artistic experimentation. This international anthology collects the comic stories of all thirty contributors from the U.S., Great Britain, France, Germany, the Netherlands, Spain, and Canada.

In addition to the complete issues of *Anarchy Comics*, the anthology features previously unpublished work by Jay Kinney and Sharon Rudahl, along with a detailed introduction by Kinney, which traces the history of the comic he founded and provides entertaining anecdotes about the process of herding an international crowd of anarchistic cats.

Contributors include: Jay Kinney, Yves Frémion, Gerhard Seyfried, Sharon Rudahl, Steve Stiles, Donald Rooum, Paul Mavrides, Adam Cornford, Spain Rodriguez, Melinda Gebbie, Gilbert Shelton, Volny, John Burnham, Cliff Harper, Ruby Ray, Peter Pontiac, Marcel Trublin, Albo Helm, Steve Lafler, Gary Panter, Greg Irons, Dave Lester, Marion Lydebrooke, Matt Feazell, Pepe Moreno, Norman Dog, Zorca, R. Diggs (Harry Driggs), Harry Robins, and Byron Werner.

"'60's counterculture, supposedly political, mostly concerned itself with hedonism and self-focused individualism, as did the underground comix it engendered. Jay Kinney's and Paul Mavrides' *Anarchy Comics*, to which all the scene's most artistically and politically adventurous creators gravitated, was an almost singular exception. Combining a grasp of Anarchy's history and principles with a genuinely anarchic and experimental approach to the form itself, Anarchy Comics represents a blazing pinnacle of what the underground was, and what it could have been. A brave and brilliant collection."
   —Alan Moore, celebrated comic writer and creator of *V for Vendetta, Watchmen, From Hell, The League of Extraordinary Gentlemen,* and numerous other comics and novels

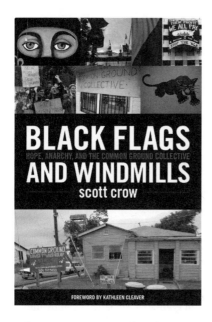

## Black Flags and Windmills
Hope, Anarchy, and the
Common Ground Collective

scott crow • Foreword by
Kathleen Cleaver
ISBN: 978-1-60486-077-1
$20.00 • 256 pages

When both levees and governments failed in New Orleans in the Fall of 2005, scott crow headed into the political storm, co-founding a relief effort called the Common Ground Collective. In the absence of local government, FEMA, and the Red Cross, this unusual volunteer organization, based on "solidarity not charity," built medical clinics, set up food and water distribution, and created community gardens. They also resisted home demolitions, white militias, police brutality, and FEMA incompetence side by side with the people of New Orleans.

crow's vivid memoir maps the intertwining of his radical experience and ideas with Katrina's reality, and community efforts to translate ideals into action. It is a story of resisting indifference, rebuilding hope amidst collapse, and struggling against the grain. *Black Flags and Windmills* invites and challenges all of us to learn from our histories, and dream of better worlds. And gives us some of the tools to do so.

> "This book is a key document in that real and a remarkable story of an activist's personal and philosophical evolution."
> —Rebecca Solnit, author of *A Paradise Built in Hell: The Extraordinary Communities That Arise in Disaster*

> "This is a compelling tale for our times."
> —Bill Ayers, author of *Fugitive Days*

> "… crow is a puppetmaster …"
> —Federal Bureau of Investigation

# Paths toward Utopia
## Graphic Explorations of Everyday Anarchism

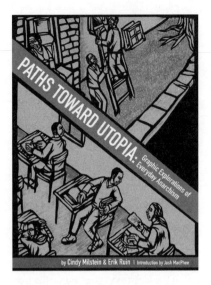

Cindy Milstein and Erik Ruin
Introduction: Josh MacPhee
ISBN: 978-1-60486-502-8
$14.95 • 120 Pages

Consisting of ten collaborative picture-essays that weave Cindy Milstein's poetic words within Erik Ruin's intricate yet bold paper-cut and scratch-board images, *Paths toward Utopia* suggests some of the here-and-now practices that prefigure, however imperfectly, the self-organization that would be commonplace in an egalitarian society. The book mines what we do in our daily lives for the already-existent gems of a freer future—premised on anarchistic ethics like cooperation and direct democracy. Its pages depict everything from seemingly ordinary activities like using parks as our commons to grandiose occupations of public space that construct do-it-ourselves communities, if only temporarily, including pieces such as "The Gift," "Borrowing from the Library," "Solidarity Is a Pizza," and "Waking to Revolution." The aim is to supply hints of what it routinely would be like to live, every day, in a world created from below, where coercion and hierarchy are largely vestiges of the past.

*Paths toward Utopia* is not a rosy-eyed stroll, though. The book retains the tensions in present-day attempts to "model" horizontal institutions and relationships of mutual aid under increasingly vertical, exploitative, and alienated conditions. It tries to walk the line between potholes and potential. Yet if anarchist and other autonomist efforts are to serve as a clarion call to action, they must illuminate how people qualitatively, consensually, and ecologically shape their needs as well as desires. They must offer stepping-stones toward emancipation. This can only happen through experimentation, by us all, with diverse forms of self-determination and self-governance, even if riddled with contradictions in this contemporary moment. As the title piece to this book steadfastly asserts, "The precarious passage itself is our road map to a liberatory society."

> "Writing-speaking differently is part of the struggle for the world we want to create and are creating, a world that moves against-and-beyond capitalism. These picture-essay-poems break the existing world both in what they say and how they say it. A fabulous book".
> —John Holloway, author of *Crack Capitalism*